John Birmingham is on the run from some mistakes
he made in Queensland. He doesn't know how those
drugs came to be inside his shoe. He grew up in Ipswich
but asks you not to hold that against him. He writes for a
wide range of publications but finds that porno mags pay
the best rates and most promptly. Some of his best friends
are lesbians. He used to work for the shadowy Office of
Special Clearances and Records within the Defence
Department but has also loaded boxes onto trucks, pulled
a few beers, and read newspapers for a clipping service.
He is kind of lazy and watches too much television. He
recommends flu tablets for hangovers.

John's other books include *How To Be A Man*
and *The Tasmanian Babes Fiasco*.

HE DIED WITH A FELAFEL

IN HIS HAND

JOHN BIRMINGHAM

DUFFY & SNELLGROVE
SYDNEY

Published by Duffy & Snellgrove
PO Box 177 Potts Point NSW 1335 Australia
info@duffyandsnellgrove.com.au

Distributed by Pan Macmillan

First published by The Yellow Press in 1994
This film edition published in 2001
2 4 6 8 10 9 7 5 3 1

Cover by Alexandra Snellgrove
Cover image courtesy of Village Roadshow
Typeset by Maggie Cooper, based on the
original design by Peter Rohen

Printed by Griffin Press

ISBN 1875989 71 4

Visit our website: www.duffyandsnellgrove.com.au

1

WHITE NIGGERS

He died with a felafel in his hand. We found him on a bean bag with his chin resting on the top button of a favourite flannelette shirt. He'd worn the shirt when we'd interviewed him for the empty room a week or so before. We were having one of those bad runs, where you seem to interview about thirty people every day and they are all total zipper heads. We really took this guy in desperation. He wasn't A-list, didn't have a microwave or anything like that, and now both he and the felafel roll were cold. Our first dead housemate. At least we got some bond off him.

We had no idea he was a junkie, otherwise we would

never have given him the room. You let one junkie in the house and you may as well let them all in. We had another secret junkie live with us once. Melissa. She was okay, but her boyfriend stole all of my CD's. Told me some Jap guy, a photographer, took them and if I went to Kinselas on Wednesday nights I could probably find

Paul

When I first got to Melbourne I was working about sixty hours a week in a new job. I had enough money to carry the rent on my two bedroom flat but after a few weeks I interviewed for someone to take the spare room. I offered it to this guy, Phil. He said he worked in the bond markets and had a heavy schedule so he'd move over a couple of evenings. First night, he cleaned the flat and dumped some gear in his room. I offered to help but he said he was okay. He crashed on the couch and I gave him a lift into the city next morning. He came round late that night and said he was going to be up past midnight. Said for me to give him a yell if he woke me up. Fine with me, I went to bed. I heard him once or twice after that but he was pretty quiet. Next morning I get up and look for Phil to see if he needs a lift. But the flat was empty. I mean empty. My stereo was gone, along with my TV, my wallet, my car keys, my car and my flatmate, Phil.

him there. Yeah right.

Melissa, on the other hand, ran a credit scam out of the same house. Months after she'd left, a couple of debt collectors came round looking for Rowan Corcoran. That was the identity she'd set up, but we didn't know that. We were very helpful, because bills had been turning up for this Corcoran prick for months. We didn't know who he was, just some mystery guy racking up

> ## Harry
>
> Ken moved out of home without understanding laundry. He'd never done any. He didn't understand the importance of rinsing. He'd give his clothes a good soaping then hang them out. I caught him trying to break his jeans across his knees once so he could get into them.

thousands of dollars in debt and sending the bills to our place. We sat the debt collectors down in the living room with a cup of tea. Showed them all the other bills that had been arriving for Mr Corcoran. When they saw that the last bill was for two Qantas tickets to America their shoulders sort of slumped. I've still got those bills. $35,000 worth.

But Melissa was okay. In fact she was a real babe. She used to steal food for the house from this restaurant she worked in. (If you're reading this Melissa, we really appreciated the food.) There were four or five of us living at Kippax Street at that stage. Everyone was on the dole or Austudy or minimum wage. The house was typical

Maria

Never move into a house
with someone who plays
The Smiths all the time.
Don't do it. I never
liked The Smiths and now
I loathe them because
it's all I hear. Three in
the morning they'll come
home and play The Smiths
at full volume and wonder
why you get into a bad
mood. Three in the
morning is the time of
choice for Smiths fans to
play their albums. The
suicide hour. Like, 'I've
been out, I've been
rejected I'm coming home
to my damp little flat to
play The Smiths and be
depressed and kill
myself'.

Darlinghurst, this huge, dark, damp terrace with yellowed ceilings, green carpet with cigarette burns and brown, torn-up furniture.

We'd sit around on Tuesday night waiting for Melissa to get home with our stolen dinner. She usually walked through the door just before *Twin Peaks* came on, so there was this nice warm feeling in the house as we all sat in front of the teev scarfing down the free stuff. On a good night, when someone's cheque had come through, we'd have a couple of beers to share round. And on a great night when someone, usually Melissa, had scored, we'd pull out the bucket bong and get completely whacked. On those nights, that nice warm feeling was really close. It wrapped you up like your Dad's old jumper, kept you safe. On those nights, you could delude yourself that share housing, which is all about deprivation and economic necessity, was really about something else: a friendly sort of half-sensible descendant of the communal ideal. But it never lasts. Never holds together. Somebody always moves on, or loses their mind, or dies with a felafel in his hand and you're on the road again.

Jeffrey!

That was the dead guy's name. It got away from me for a minute there, but I knew it started with a 'J'. He died watching *Rage* with the sound turned down. One of the hip young inner-city cops who turned up to investigate said he probably snuffed it half way through the hot one hundred. Just like a junkie. There was a nightclub stamp on his wrist, bruises up and down his arm. The felafel's chilli and yoghurt sauce had leaked from the roll and run down his hand in little white rivulets. For a brief, perverse moment it seemed to me that he himself had sprung a leak, a delicate stream of liquid heroin escaping from the seams of his fingers.

I've seen a hundred lives pass through the bleary kind of sleep-deprived landscape of a dozen different share houses, but Jeffrey's was the only one that ever fetched up and died on a bean bag. The others all moved along on their own weird trajectories. They were never still. Everybody was constantly mobile or wanting to be – moving targets, random drifters and people whose lives rested on nothing more stable than inertia. White niggers every one. Some of them now work for gigantic weapons corporations or drug cartels. They've got these incredible lives. Jet travel. Credit cards. Respect, even fear, from those top-hatted guys who stand in front of the Hyatt. But if they were housemates of mine, I've seen them bludging meals from the Krishnas. Or sitting on the lounge room floor in home-brand underwear with all the windows blacked out and hundreds of candles pushing back the dark. Not doing much. Just sitting there. Or smashing five hundred empty beer bottles into a million jagged pieces on the kitchen floor while greying mincemeat patties slowly peel away from the ceiling … slowly, slowly, slowly … then plop – impaled on the waiting fangs of glass below. Or sitting in front of the television for two days straight, with giant frilled lizards clinging to their shoulders, a bowl of magic mushrooms by their feet, their weeping bloodshot eyes the shape of little rectangles.

Madness, as one flatmate of mine used to say with just a hint of satisfaction in his voice. Things get out of control all the time in share houses. It's not just a matter of the rent slipping behind, or the washing piling up. People flip over the line. Way over. I know about this. Been there myself a couple of times. One place, Duke Street – home of the smashed stubbies and falling patties – was nothing but a madhouse. A huge rambling kind of place, an ex-brothel, we all thought, because there were so many rooms in there. A lot of them looked like they had been jerry-built at some stage. Bedrooms where bedrooms shouldn't ought to be and so on. We were paying $11 a week each between the ten or eleven of us living there. We were never completely sure of the number because of the

Karen

Living with other people you start off in that nice accommodating phase. 'Okay we're going to get on'. You try really hard. It's all going to be great. You buy stuff together, you talk, you share, you bond over instant coffee in the kitchen late at night. And then it starts to get a little cramped, becomes too much. Your dope's getting smoked. Your car is always getting borrowed. The phone kitty never makes it above a handful of coins even though you keep filling it with change. You don't want to put the effort in anymore. It's almost like an ill-considered marriage. All this shit comes up like a marriage like, 'You're supposed to be loyal to me because I live with you.' Even if they're wrong. So you start thinking divorce. You're not talking. You're knifing each other to your mutual friends, trying to entangle them in a complicated network of alliances to suit your ends. Then you're not even thinking divorce, you're thinking pre-emptive strike. Who's going to run up a thousand bucks on the phone and skip town at midnight leaving the other holding the bill.

Susan

An English girl whom I didn't get on with very well put some dead fish up the chimney in my bedroom and then went out for the night with some of the other girls who lived there. While they were out she had a fight with one of them. She came home steaming, marched into my room, while I was there, took the fish out of my chimney and put it in the other girl's bed.

continual drop-ins and disappearances and the strange case of Satomi Tiger.

I just know you're thinking – what the hell is a Satomi Tiger? Well, we're sitting on the lino floor of the living room one night – actually we had two living rooms in this weird house, but we turned the other one into a basketball court – and we're watching teev, as usual. And this Japanese girl walks in wearing these audacious tiger-striped pants and a poo-brown imitation dead fur thing. 'Good Ev-en-ing,' she says. 'I move in now.' And that was all. She had no other English. She drops a wad of cash on the teev and wanders off to find a room. We're all just sitting there thinking 'What the hell is this?' But then again, she's dropped this wad on the teev so who cares?

We found out later that Satomi Tiger had met our invisible flatmate Tim on his last trip to Asia, the one which ended up with him being investigated for espionage and committed to an insane asylum in Hong Kong. You can see

Tim in the mini-series *Bangkok Hilton*. He plays three different bit parts, most notably that of a drunken buffoon in a boat. A frighteningly accurate performance. Tim escaped from the asylum with the help of a friend, also called Tim, but he was always a little elsewhere afterwards. He'd met Satomi Tiger in Japan and invited her to visit him in Queensland. She took him up on the offer. Only thing was, we never really knew where Tim was at any given moment. When Satomi Tiger arrived, rumour had him cutting cane in the north. Whatever. It didn't bother her, and it didn't really bother us. It was that kind of house. The set-up with the rent, for instance, was mondo suspicious. We'd send a cash cheque every two or three weeks to this post office box in the western suburbs, deep in serial killer territory. We'd never get any receipts but we never got any hassles either. There was a phone number to call in emergencies, which we used when the bathroom looked like it was going to fall off the end of the house one time, but there would only be this spooky message at the other end.

'There's no one here,' click, brrrrrrrrrr ....

At that stage, I'd quit my job in Canberra and was kicking around Brisbane, wasting my life again. Duke Street seemed the perfect place for it. The floating population, the lack of furniture, the crazy tilting floors, the freight train line which ran through the back yard, the hallucinogenic mushrooms in the front yard, the tree which grew through

Jane

I had a hairdressing flatmate who had a tribe of
dumb hairdressing friends. Every Friday and
Saturday night they'd come around to tease and
spray each other before going out. I came home
early one Saturday from a horror date which I'd
mainly gone on to avoid the hairdressers. My other
flatmate had taken the TV into her bedroom and I
went in there to tell her about the date. While
we're talking we notice this funny smell. We both
thought 'Oh that's really weird. It must be coming
in the windows or something.' We started watching a
movie. But this smell just got stronger and
stronger. It was like a burning chemical smell, it
really got into the nostrils. We're going around
checking all the points and electricals. Finally we
went into her room. There was a cord going into
her bed. When I pulled the doona back I briefly
recognised a plastic curling iron before the oxygen
got it and - whoof! fucking fire. We grabbed the
burning doona and ran into the kitchen which was
tiled, started stomping on it, throwing water and
so on. Totally spun out. The hairdresser got home
at three in the morning, pissed off her face, woke
us up and accused us of setting fire to her bed.

the bedroom window, the constant low grade harassment by the Department of Social Security, the week long drinking binges, the horror, the horror.

Early in my stay there, I took a four week job as a typist with the Department of Primary Industry. They had these reports that were seven years overdue. I'm not joking. They stressed this point to me. Seven years. Probably dog years too. So I'm bashing away on a word processor, getting into the Zen of typing because it's so dull if I actually stop to think what I'm doing, my head will implode and I'll be this sultana-headed guy walking around town. Anyway, after a while I look around the typing pool and I get this huge Fear. This Fear grabs me by the heart and squeezes like a bastard for three days straight. It's saying This Is Your Life. So I enrol in Law at Queensland University.

God, I hated it. A few weeks into semester the first assignment is due. I've already missed a few classes and my notes aren't that great. I'm surrounded by these carnivorous teenagers, fresh-smelling, label-wearing, beady-eyed little ratbastards who never lend me their notes. On the day I've set aside to do this assignment, I can't find anything, not even the question sheet and I flip over the line. I start screaming. It sounds like something from the jungle or a subterranean prison for the criminally insane where all the inmates have devolved into these lower forms. They don't even look human any more and they're taking messages straight from the brain stem, primitive reptilian urgings.

I've got this working through me. I kick a hole in the wall and pick up a golf club and charge into the living room and start laying about me and letting go with more of the monster screeches. Well the other guys in the house, they've been there. They sort of hang back and watch the show. Get a beer from the fridge, that sort of thing. And eventually I do calm down. I'm not that fit, and my arms go tired and I deflate like an old balloon. I realise everybody is watching me, grinning hugely. I shrug. Means nothing. An hour later we found Satomi Tiger hiding in a cupboard. She'd never stay in the same room as me after that.

Madness, you see. Things getting out of control. It's one of the constants of share housing. Now I'll allow that most of the time it doesn't get to the stage of kicking out walls and terrifying obscure tiger-suited Japanese girls, but it's always there, a sort of chaotic potential snaking about under the surface of things, rearing its head only briefly in the course of arguments over phone bills or cleaning up.

Like, I used to share a flat with a bank clerk called Derek. Derek the bank clerk pitched a tent, literally, on the living room floor. The house budget needed one more rent payer but had no more rooms, and Derek the bank clerk needed a place to stay but was kind of a tight-arse about money. So he builds this tent thing in the corner of the living room and pays half-rent. Crawls into this thing at night. Crawls out of it in the morning. A real fringe-dwelling bank clerk. It worked for a while. But Derek was very territorial. Used to gradually creep that tent across the floor into the television-watching area. Liked to poke his head out of the flaps and watch the ABC. During the day, when he was gone, I'd push it back. At night, he'd creep it out again. It started small at first, a few inches one way, a few inches back. But the confrontation went on. He'd jump his border out a whole foot. I'd push it back a metre. He'd take two metres. I'd break a tent pole. And the whole time, never a word was spoken. It was a lucky thing we didn't keep guns in the house. You could feel it moving towards a bloody climax, but fortunately the bank transferred him and this taxi driver moved in. We said, 'No tents taxi driver, just throw a mattress here on the floor.' That was cool with him. He liked being in the centre of things. But it raised another problem, made it difficult to keep the flat tidy.

I have to jump a couple of houses here and tell you that the worst place I ever lived, absolutely the dirtiest filthiest place, was King Street. A rat died in the living room at King Street and we didn't know. There was at least six inches of compacted crap between our feet and the floor. Old Ratty must have crawled in there and died of pleasure. A visitor uncovered him while groping about for a beer. I don't want to go into detail on King Street yet but remind me later to tell you about the open door policy in the toilet, and the pubic hair competition and how the kitchen got so bad we had to do all of our cooking in the back yard.

You shouldn't get the idea that all share houses are like that though. I've lived in some beautiful places. Really I have. Mostly they stayed that way because women lived there too. Not always, but mostly. I don't want to be sexist about this, but there's something about men living together that unleashes the Beast.

Gay guys are okay to live with on that score. They're hyper-clean. Problem is, they're also hypersensitive about the gay thing. I had a housemate come out on me once. This guy, Dirk, appeared in the living room at one or two in the morning when I was putting the moves on this girl Nina, who also lived there. There were tear tracks on his face as he stood there staring at us. I was giving this Nina a foot massage at the time, I mean, really giving her the works so I didn't notice him at first. But he starts snuffling and kind of whimpering and we spin around. I've got this girl's foot in my lap and there's old Dirk, sort of staring and snuffling and of course I think, uh oh, old Dirk's got a thing for Nina. The moment's destroyed as you can imagine, and then Dirk says, 'I'm gay.'

Whew! What a relief.

Now I can see old Dirk is doing it tough. And I like to think myself a broad-minded sort of guy. So I say to

SAVE MONEY. EAT LESS

him, 'Hey. Always thought you were.' At the time, it passes for male sensitivity. Anyway Nina sits through the horrors of the night with him and I get to go to bed dreaming of her soft, milky white feet. I ask you, who got the raw end of the deal? Funny thing is, Nina and Dirk hated each other. They were always having these knock-down drag-out scream-o-ramas about stuff like whether the tuna chunks went in the cupboard or the fridge.

Nina moved out shortly after that, so this other girl Emma and I got to live with Dirk while he was coming to terms with his sexuality. The trouble wasn't with him being gay (we did pass a house by-law that banned kissing and fondling on the lounge room couch, but it applied to all sexual orientations). The trouble was that we didn't care he was gay. So we'd say these brutal things which he'd pick up on his sophisticated gay radar. We'd say, 'How about cleaning the shower, Dirk?' and he'd decode it as, 'You filthy little arse-bandits should all be nailed to a tree.'

Do you think we could get old Dirk to clean that bathroom? No way. He wasn't buying into any heterofascist sterility conspiracy. 'Gay men are dying,' he'd screech at a bemopped Em on cleaning day. He eventually inherited half a million dollars and moved out to set up a gay men's retreat in northern Queensland. Hope his gay brothers put him straight about the cleaning thing.

Don't know how Dirk would have coped with finding Jeffrey the junkie all cold and blue and sprawled over the bean bag. An actual dead guy as opposed to the rhetorical gay ones which littered his post-closet conversation. Seeing as Dirk never surfaced before *Donahue*, I guess it would have been academic even if he and Jeffrey had lived under the same roof. One thing's for sure. He wouldn't have cleaned up the mess, so he wouldn't have found the thousand bucks Jeffrey had stashed away in his room. The cops told us to stay out of there until the science guys had come around to check it out properly but we snuck in about ten minutes after they left. It didn't take very long to find the cash rolled up and hidden away in the battery compartment of his ghetto blaster and since he'd lied to us about being a junkie and brought a world of hassles down on our home we figured it was only fair that Jeffrey make this posthumous contribution to the kitty.

a modern aesthetic

Ted

<u>ON LIVING WITH MARXISTS</u>

My friend Ted says Marxists are
worse than junkies. You know, you
let one in, you let the whole
anarcho-syndicalist commune in, and then
your little home isn't the warm and
friendly place you escape to at day's
end. It's a brave challenge to the
dominant paradigm of crypto-fascist
domestic enslavement. Until the washing
has to be done. Then it always seems
to be Ted's turn.

TED NOW WORKS
FOR THE DEPARTMENT OF ADMINISTRATIVE
AFFAIRS.

Adam was a full-on Marxist, originally from Broken Hill. He's probably lecturing in English now. While I was living with him he would interpret everything according to a Marxist line. When we went shopping you'd get a little diatribe on each product. If this were a Marxist society, for instance, one-litre bottles of Spring Valley orange juice would be just the right height to hold dry fettucine. But because this is a capitalist society they make the Spring Valley bottle two and a half centimetres too short to store your dry fettucine. They do this on purpose.

Adam said he wouldn't read a book if it did not have the word Marxism in the index. He fucked every woman he could get his hands on whilst professing to be a liberated feminist man. Big, flabby, white-bodied old Adam would wander about in a sarong with his willy hanging out because he wasn't part of any sexually oppressive state mechanism or anything.

He had a big mouldy chair in the corner which he would sit in half-naked, overseeing the room. There was a reading light carefully arranged behind the chair to put him into an enigmatic perspective for anybody who walked into the room. He bought Freddy the tabby cat to sit on the arm of

this chair and complete the illusion.
Blofeld with his cat, but in a sarong.
Freddy was meant to be an aloof cat, sort of
a guardian. But sadly Freddy was very
affectionate and he'd interrupt Adam's
reading by purring and headbutting him all
the time. He'd also bring grasshoppers into
the house to terrify Rodney the gay guy. We
came home one night and found Rodney pinned
to the door, screaming, with Freddy sitting
a few feet in front of him crunching away on
a grasshopper.
The cat had no idea Rodney didn't want it.
He must have taken Rodney's theatrics for
excitement, because he followed him around
with this twitching corpse until we got home
and rescued him.
Rodney was also on the Left but he was in
the drug taking, campy gay faction. Rodney
had just come from a house in Taringa where
they had set aside one day a week as Nude
Day. Even visitors had to get their gear off
and leave it at the door. One Nude Day they
got stoned and decided that it would be
completely cool to watch a glass fall off
the balcony onto the path below. They
dropped this glass, got really excited when
it shattered. So the house's entire crockery
collection went over after it and was left
in a pile in the driveway. The next morning

they didn't have any bowls for breakfast.
Rodney and Adam didn't get on too well
because Adam was very much into being a
bloke. He thought Rodney a little frivolous.
Whereas Rodney was all for fighting the
revolution aided by copious quantities of
drugs and condoms. He thought Adam a little
uptight. These two factions then contended
for control of the house. The serious young
stick insects Stalinist discussion group and
the drug-fucked, dick-sucking, no-hopers
collective.

Rodney won in the end. Adam moved out
because he just couldn't hack it. The
telling blow came when Rodney brought home
about seven or eight of his gay drug buddies
and they all piled into the bathroom, which
was next to Adam's bedroom. They lit dozens
of candles, filled up the bathtub, got naked
and got into it. They were stoned out of
their heads, yelling and singing awful Billy
Bragg songs while Rodney played along on his
piano. He'd play for a while then go back to
cavorting in the tub. About three in the
morning Adam came out of his room to yell at
them to shut the fuck up and start acting
their age. He bawled them out for a good ten
minutes but when he got back to his room
three of them were fucking in his bed.

THE WILD THING

I can listen to my flatmates have sex for ever. I once lurked in a lounge room for a whole weekend on the slim chance that two flatmates were holed up in the upstairs front bedroom, and that if I waited long enough, I might hear them at it. They were young and desperately trying to be cool about it, but the signs had been there for a week – meaningful glances, late night teev, foot massages, the standard routine. And there was no way I was letting them off without some heavy duty, gargoyle-style voyeurism on my part. When you're young and blameworthy, there's this circuit in your brain that's always pushing you to go for the end zone, and I did – made a quick trek to the 7-11, bought both the weekend papers, a fruit loaf, fresh coffee, and camped out in the living room, directly downstairs from the point of maximum creaking and moaning.

Other flatmates looked outside the house for their mistakes. Melissa, you remember her, the credit scam queen, she was a great one for bringing home these rough-headed bastards with tattoos and biker boots and the stench of failure about them. She was a safe sex girl. You'd hear her through the bedroom door and all the way down the hall – 'Just put it on you fucking dickhead' – and these guys would grudgingly comply, slap on the latex and wake up in the morning to discover that Melissa spends the best part of her daylight hours asleep. Sleep is her natural state of being. These hellmen would wake up, take in her chainsaw

Stella

I walked in on a flatmate one day. His girlfriend was sitting naked on his desk with her legs spread wide apart. I reversed out at top speed really embarrassed. He came and knocked on my door later. He said 'It's not what it looks at all. I'm actually a virgin. I've had this girlfriend for two years but we don't do anything. She just comes around once a week, sits herself up on the desk and shows me what I can't have.'

snores and figure they could slip away, sneak out of the house and avoid those always awkward post-coital negotiations. So they'd pull on their gear in careful silence and pad downstairs to where I'm waiting in the lounge room, pretending to read the papers because it is absolutely my favourite thing to catch these guys out. The good mannered ones might throw a grunt at me, but mostly they'd steam through the lounge, heading for the front door and freedom. They'd fling it open. And freeze. Because the house has got these heavy cast iron security gates over all the windows and doors. There's this great pause as the hellmen realise they are locked in with me, the dog and the girl upstairs. There's always a few seconds while these ugly bastards stare at the bars. I'm biting my cheeks to keep a straight face when they come back into the lounge. They always say something like, 'Uh, you got a key ... man?'

'Sorry. Lost mine. Melissa's got one though.'

I got a taste for this sort of thing in the first place I ever lived out of home – the Boulevarde, an old off-campus unit block in Brisbane. The place had light blue walls which used to sweat at night and shake whenever a truck drove past. I moved in with Warren and Mel, a young couple I knew from my high school days. It was pretty exciting for all of us. They had never been able to sleep together at their parents' homes, and I'd never been under the same roof as two people I knew, for a fact, were having sex. Parents don't count, unless you're a pervert.

It wasn't all fruit loaf and voyeurism though. I came home one day and found the flat deserted but feeling odd. Things seemed out of place but not in any identifiable way. It took a few minutes before I realised my coffee table had disappeared. When I asked Mel about it, she blushed, muttered something about Warren, and disappeared into her room. The table had always been wobbly, and as Warren was a carpenter's apprentice I thought he might have taken it off to be fixed. In fact, he had taken it off to the dump. My flatmates had been coupling on my cheap chip-board coffee table that afternoon, and it had collapsed under the onslaught. I privately thought it was kind of cool, but they moved out shortly after. Said something about privacy. Andy, the med student who took over their room, had no such hang-ups. He was happy to let you perch outside his door while he worked his magic inside. He was a handsome cad, but kind of dopey for a future surgeon. He liked to walk around with his food, but would forget he was holding it. You'd watch him tip a plate of spaghetti towards the floor, tipping it and tipping it, and you'd think – 'Surely he's going to tip it back the other way soon.' But no. It'd slide off and hit the carpet and his shoes. Plop. His eyes would go wide, and then after a pause, he'd chuckle just like Goofy. The other med students called him Dr Death. Once, over the course of a fortnight, he invited three different girls to a college ball and only realised what he had done on the day of the event. He cancelled one date, but thought he could keep the others apart. He couldn't of course, and the third girl turned up anyway. It was a disaster. A few weeks later he bedded all three of them anyway, one after the other. The first girl turned up at three. He was rid of her by four. Then the second arrived, unannounced, with a couple of suitcases and a pure wool sweater she'd knitted for him. I answered the door and she brushed straight past me. 'I'm moving in,' she said. Andy had her and the suitcases out of the flat by six. He kept the sweater and gave it to the last girl who showed up just after dinner.

Only ever lived with one other guy like that. Downstairs Ivan. He kept a string of girls going, but apart from roaring like a bear when he took them in the shower, he was a very private kind of guy. The Sisterhood did for him in the end. He was cheating on Sally, his steady girl, a stunning babe. I didn't understand him at all. She was only allowed around to the house on Wednesday, Friday and Saturday nights. The other nights were reserved for study, he told her. In fact, they were reserved for noisy, vertical sex in our bathroom with a succession of nameless nightclubbing bimbos who used their ankles for earrings and left before dawn.

Gina and Veronica, the girls of the house, put Sally straight on the whole deal when she came around one afternoon. She was in a state. She'd heard things around town. The three of them fronted Downstairs Ivan that night. Said they had a few bones to pick with him. I backed off straight away, thinking, 'Uh oh, here it comes,' and it did – Sally and the house girls nailed Downstairs in the hallway and unleashed the most frightening bitchkrieg I've ever seen in ten years of share housing. It went all night, like the bombing of Dresden. I almost felt sorry for the poor bastard when they finished with him. They worked him over so badly that Sally had no choice but to clear her stuff out of his room and refuse to speak to him ever again, despite the fact she adored him like the girl-with-a-mind-of-her-own in all of the Elvis Presley films. There was no resisting the power of the Sisterhood – Gina and Veronica told her about the bimbos, the bathroom, the moaning at 3.00am. They told her she was too good for him, she could have any man, she should teach him a lesson, she should cut up his clothes, get a new boyfriend, move interstate and put it about that he was a dud root. All of which she did. She had no choice really.

The whole time, I was sitting in the cramped little airing cupboard I used for a writing room. Downstairs would occasionally appear at my door shaking his head and scratching his Judd Nelson goatee. 'She dropped me,' he'd say. He couldn't believe it. Couldn't come at the idea. She didn't even want to hear his side of the story. 'Why?' he asked. 'Why?' Who was to say? Not me, that's for sure. He moved out a week or two later. He shook my hand before he left, but pointedly ignored Gina and Veronica. They didn't care. There was real loathing between them. Actually, there was some real loathing from me too when we totalled the prick's contribution to our phone bill. One thousand dollars. Most of it in desperate, crazed international phonecalls, the last three days he was there.

Other than Warren and Mel getting married, and me being entertained, I can't think of anything good that has ever come of the sex lives of my numerous flatmates. Friendships crash and burn all the time because of sex, so it's not surprising that the tenuous equilibrium of a share house can be disturbed by it. I lost a great house in Canberra when one flatmate developed a case of unrequited love for another. Zoe and Michael.

By day, Michael was a salaryman, a marketing manager with General Dynamics. He favoured the Country Road catalogue. Little glasses, the tweed jacket, the tie just right, the clouds of after-shave trailing behind him, killing insects like napalm. Michael was an instant taste guy. He moved in, needed some furniture, went to Ikea and whacked down the Visa. Bought the big black cupboard, the big potted plant – which died from lack of water – and the big, big, big black bed for entertaining. Ladies were enticed into the lotus trap by the lilting strains of Madame Butterfly on his big black stereo.

Zoe had an ex-boyfriend who used to beat up on her. She missed him terribly. Don't ask me why. She'd get distressed over this loser and bring out the Simon and Garfunkel tapes. She'd drop a couple of Panadols, take her ghetto blaster into the living room about three in the morning, lie down and howl along with *Bridge Over Troubled Water* while I was four feet away in the next room, trying to sleep. After a fistful of sleepless nights I resolved that if I ever got to meet this ex-boyfriend, this tragic, hapless, girl-beating oaf, I was going to kick his teeth in, if only for the tapes and the sound of Zoe snoring on the floor.

Anyway, we have a spare room. Michael moves in and Zoe goes on the make for him. Michael is a mover, a man with money and cred and she falls for him. Nothing is too much trouble. Michael couldn't clean. Didn't even consider it. Wasn't on his agenda. So Zoe looked after that. In the nine months he lived there, he never once washed his towels. But he emerged from his stinking sink hole of a bedroom every morning, perfectly clean.

Zoe's first shock came early. One morning, a week after he moved in, a strange woman emerged from the sinkhole behind him. She was explained away as a lost friend from out of town. Nowhere to stay. She looked kind of lost when she surfaced after eight hours of Mme Butterfly, but that hiccup aside, Zoe set about the wooing of Michael. He was new to Canberra, and Zoe was throwing her cards on the table, showing him round, inviting friends over to ease him into the scene. She organised candle-lit dinners with the Spinsters Club – her friends Katerina and Vicky – with Michael on the menu. The plan was for Zoe to finally put the word on Michael during a big night on the town. His mates were even invited along as dates for the Spinsters Club. Unfortunately, at the last moment, Michael couldn't make it. And then Katerina cancelled. And the next morning, Katerina crawls out of Michael's bedroom after a night of the Butterfly. Trouble is, the whole time, Zoe's room is right next door to Michael's – their beds are wall to wall with only half an inch of wood between them, and Zoe's listening to everything. And it's more than she can bear. She's tearing down the hallway, hammering on Michael's door screaming 'Turn it down. I'm trying to get some sleep,' and I'm somewhere out there in the dark, my head thumping with tension and the knowledge that the days of this house are numbered.

So Katerina was out of the Spinsters Club. Little alliances formed and reformed. Michael would ask, 'John, what goes on? What's happened?' And I'd explain that he was stepping out with Zoe's best friend. And Michael would go 'My God, you know it's got nothing to do with her.' Then Zoe would appear in my room and whisper that Michael was a bastard and a prick and what did I think, what were we going to do? Could I do something? Speak to him maybe? Make him move out? I thought I might turn all of this to my advantage; get Michael to clean up, make Zoe deep six the Simon and Garfunkel tapes, but in the end, Michael moved out and Zoe took up gardening.

I should have got the hell out myself, but as usual, I hung around. I always hang around – I'm always there, living below my means for any number of reasons, be it finishing my pointless degree in Queensland, or working a dumb job in Canberra to pay off that degree. But between Canberra and my house in Kippax Street, Darlinghurst – which is like the definitive, King Hell, Thousand Year Reich of share house experience – things got interesting.

I led a dissolute, basically itinerant life. Not an eating-out-of-dumpsters, sleeping-under-bridges sort of life, you understand. More of a daytime TV, skipping out on phone bills, deep fried home-brand fish finger sandwiches sort of life. I lived in a lot of places and racked up a lot of flatmates in those three or four years. A dozen houses, sixty people, something like that. The figures are inflated by one place I stayed in for less than a week before doing a runner after a couple of Goths painted the living room black and hung an old goat's head over the fireplace. Said it was for a sacrifice that night.

Gothic design tip: dead things are so cool they just have to be nailed to the wall. The freshly rendered goat's head actually replaced a pressed duck which had been there for two years. Somebody had found it in Chinatown, semi-cooked and semi-glazed, then pressure-sealed in a vacuum

Sharon

I didn't know anyone when I first got to Melbourne
so I stayed with my boyfriend. I really needed
some space so I moved in with this girl, Brooke.
The flat was cramped but it was cheap and it had a
view of the beach. I'd been there four or five
days, no hassles, when I went out with my
boyfriend one night. He came back and stayed over.
The next day I get home from work and Brooke says
'Your boyfriend stayed last night.' I apologised
for not introducing her, but said she'd been in
bed. She just stared at me and said 'You go to
Hell for that sort of thing. I don't want to live
with a sinner'. And then she went apeshit, screaming, 'Don't you know what you're doing is wrong?
The Lord has a special place in Hell for the
fornicators. I couldn't bear the guilt of having
a fornicator under the roof of the House of the
Lord.' I spun out, struck dumb. She was psychotic
for a few minutes, yelling all this fire and
brimstone stuff and how there was no hope for me.
And then she switched totally, went dead calm and
said, 'But if you change your ways I'm willing
to let you stay.' I moved out the next day. I'd
been there less than a week but she kept a
month's rent.

bag. This duck was already rotten, twisted, half burned and bereft of feathers when they nailed it over the fireplace. Over the years the bag lost its seal and the duck started coming out and making its way down the wall.

I'd thought about cutting out earlier when I woke to the sound of this pair of Goths having sex on the floor next to me, and again when I discovered that although the water was connected, the kitchen sink wasn't – you pulled the plug and it just spilled out onto the floor. But Satan's living room did it for me.

You get these moments, these Satan's lounge room, goat's head moments, and you wonder what forces delivered you to this place at this time. It's as though your life travels through this complex grid where stuff happens, like you date this girl or you go to that movie or you come home to find a goat's head nailed to the wall, and a little point of light plots the event on the grid. All the points are woven together by this weird mathematical program that determines the course of your life and the future – each little moment, each point of light, driven along by the falling numbers of some impenetrable logarithm.

Hmmm. Guess I'd better get back to it.

The Boulevarde was advertised as a top floor three bedroom apartment. The third bedroom was actually down in the basement garage. Mel and I took the two rooms upstairs and banished Tom, the quiet engineering student, to the carpark. He didn't mind it down there. He pulled apart a security light switch and tapped into the unit block's power supply. After that, our power bills were paid by the body corporate and we ran every light and appliance we owned twenty-four hours a day. Tom, who is a vice president with an international airline nowadays, seemed to live off the land back then. His success in making jam from the blackberries he collected down by the river led us to plant a choko vine down there. We managed one harvest, but nobody in the house ate chokos and they rotted under the kitchen sink. His favourite meal was fish finger pie. (Roll six fish fingers and two cheese sticks into a lot of dough. Bake.) On special occasions, he'd make raspberry pudding, a poisonous blend of red cordial and custard powder. It looked like blood soup and tasted like a bowl full of water with human hair soaking in it.

I learned something about the value of people in that flat. Mel's boyfriend Warren was just a carpenter's apprentice from Cloncurry. He was never going to read any Foucault, and seeing as I had a crush on his girlfriend, we were probably never going to get along. But we did. Warren had a good soul and he pulled cones like a trooper – our relationship was based around these intangible moments of stoned camaraderie, where we would talk … sort of. And if the conversation became a little stilted, we could always stimulate it artificially – a cone before breakfast, a few cones at lunch, a joint with dinner, two or three more cones with MASH. I had to cut back on the smoke after fading out during an early morning

Tricia

I lived downstairs in a terrace. There were two boys upstairs. I could always hear this scratching. It was driving me mad so I got one of the boys to come outside and try and find what it was. We looked all around but couldn't find it for ages. It just went on and on. Scritch scritch scritch. Then one day rather than going outside the house we happened to look out of a top floor window and saw this little kid from next door, we called him Naughty David. He was scraping away at the wall with a stick. He'd drilled a hole in the wall outside my room to watch me in the nuddy.

Chinese class and snapping back into a room where everybody was speaking Cantonese. I had a major panic attack, thought I'd smoked so much I'd lost the power to comprehend speech.

Paranoia was a part of my every waking moment in those days. Queensland had some monster drug laws back then. Still does. I once turned the corner to find two cop cars pulled into our driveway, blue lights strobing in the night. I fell into the bush by the side of the road and waited for them to lead my flatmates away to a mandatory life sentence in some gulag out west. The cops pulled out after fifteen minutes. Alone. When I got the courage up to crawl back into the flat, it was smoke-choked as usual but nobody was home. Turned out the gang had gone for pizza. We never found out what those cops were doing there. Warren suggested they may have slipped through a rip in the fabric of the universe, from an alternate reality where we really did get busted. But he was about six cones over the line at the time. They were more likely responding to a noise complaint. The Boulevarde had a trumpet player who just would not give up. And these Vietnamese students who'd sing along with a tape of Olivia Newton-John's 'Physical' at seven o'clock every night.

That was about the time Warren and Mel totalled my coffee table, moved out and got married. Tom and I wore brown tuxedos with fat lapels to the reception. Andy the med student took their place and you already know most of what there is to know about him. Except that his mother had this habit of sneaking into the flat to clean it while we were away. I caught her once. Came home a day early from a trip to my parents' place and found the front door wide open, a vacuum cleaner going inside. Neither Tom nor Andy was supposed to be there. And we didn't own a vacuum cleaner. Clean burglars? Hoovering up the evidence? I tip-toed in and found Andy's mum had cleaned the entire flat, my room included. I wasn't too sure I approved of this, but it didn't happen again. Absent-mindedness ran in their family. Andy's sister wasted an Ampol station a few weeks later – drove into the restaurant without getting out of the car. Andy had to move home to help pay for the damage. (Just one footnote on him. He married one of the three girls from that outstanding afternoon of passion – the one who arrived with her suitcases and the knitted jumper. She was a nurse. They split up a few years later and both asked for transfers to get as far away from each other as possible. They were both sent to the Cocos Islands.)

Derek the bank clerk replaced Andy the med student. He didn't build his tent in that particular flat, he actually had a room there. The tent came later. He was a funny little dude. Went to the toilet about eight or nine times a night. Thought this was normal. Wondered why he never bumped into us the same way he bumped into the members of his family all the time at home. Derek didn't have much in the way of a life back then. He'd put in eight hours at the bank and come home to arrange his collection of travel brochures. He read travel brochures the way most people watch television. All his money went into saving for the trip he'd take at the end of the year and all his energy went into planning that trip to the smallest detail. So even with Derek in the house there was never too much money around. We seemed to survive week to week, but there were plenty of moments when the bills outstripped our income by an impossible margin. One week we had twenty dollars between the three of us, so we bought two family-sized jumbo cans of Spam, a bag of onions and some beer. We fried up the Spam and onion, made this big ugly mess and

ate every mouthful because we were so hungry. I
investigated a rumour that IVF programs paid twenty
dollars a pop for semen donations but found it to be
baseless.

We split from that flat in December. Derek the bank
clerk was off to Japan for a month. Tom and I were off to
minimum wage holiday jobs and our parents' homes to save
the thousand dollars we were allowed to earn before the
government cut off our $37 a week Austudy grant. And our
yearly $2.10 travel allowance. The flat we took the

Keiran

I once shared with some guys and this very, very
strange woman. She had this really violent, ongoing
and intermittent affair with a truckie. She used to
beat the crap out of him after drunken nights out.
Took to him with whatever came to hand. A chair, a
claw hammer, anything. That was, of course, in
between one night stands. You'd be watching the
Sunday program on TV and the bleary-eyed Beast (as
we called her) would wander out to vomit off the
verandah. Then, about ten minutes later she'd boot
out the latest guy in her clutches - a different
guy every weekend. We tried to warn them but they
wouldn't listen. They'd ring constantly and turn up
with flowers.

following February was, as I mentioned, a two room affair. Hence Derek's tent in the living room. When the bank transferred him he asked me if I could arrange to move his miniature Indian village. I said sure, and threw it off our third storey patio an hour after he'd driven away.

Martin the paranoid wargamer replaced Derek the bank clerk, but only for two weeks. Martin would ask you to play wargames with him four or five times an hour, becoming increasingly moodier as the refusals mounted up. He was also a pig. Tom caught him messing up the lounge room just after it had been cleaned. Scattering Mars bar wrappers and soiled underwear about like fertiliser pods in a promising garden. When we hinted that he wasn't welcome anymore, he accused us of trying to poison him, just like his previous flatmates. We actually did consider poisoning him, but he was a runty little specimen and it proved easier to frog-march him out the door and toss his stuff off the patio, where it joined the pile of mouldering tent debris.

Taylor the taxi driver dropped his swag in the space left vacant by Martin's sudden exit. It was kind of cool having our own cabbie. He had an account at a strip club in the Valley, a basement firetrap with cracked mirror balls and one slightly hunch-backed topless waitress whom Taylor was courting with the few lines of Shakespeare he remembered from high school English. They served meals in this place and he'd drive us into town at three in the morning for video games and greasy food binges. Things ran smoothly until the landlady came around for an inspection. We knew she was coming and had hidden Taylor's stuff away as there was only supposed to be two of us living there. But she was a sharp-eyed old biddy and when she saw the three neatly lined-up pairs of differently sized shoes she tumbled to our scam. She was pretty cool about it. Said we could stay, but we'd have to pay full rent for three people. That was never going to happen so we loaded our minimal gear into Taylor's cab and split for that old reliable share house bolthole. Our parents.

STUNNING

DECOR

CHOICE

Brown Couch

<u>AAAH. LEISURE!</u>

Trip to the snow this year? A little snorkelling around the Reef? Maybe some time on a genuine homestead?

Yes these are all fine ideas. But have you ever considered the <u>Brown Couch</u>?

Our special four seater model comes with a complimentary set of Paisley Pillows, an Old Newspaper and a Remote Control for the TV*.

Why waste valuable time and money when everything you ever wanted in a holiday is available in the <u>LUXURY</u> and <u>CONVENIENCE</u> of your own living room.

THE BROWN COUCH.
FIRST CHOICE OF THE CHOOSEY.

*TV sold separately.

THE BEAST

PJ's life revolved around Cold Chisel, karate, beer and babes. He was a country boy. Loved his fish fingers. Favourite recipe: three deep-fried fish fingers on fried bread with fried cheese and two fried eggs, still runny, forked open and covered with tomato sauce. You could eat three of those suckers and stay within the tightest budget. Of course if you did get through three, your heart would explode and you'd die.

Milo's life revolved around his car, his mum, beer and the Buzzcocks. He had a weakness for generic brand meat pies. You couldn't trust the bastard with shopping duty because he'd come back with twenty of these family-size, Woolies Own bowel-cramping horrors. Milo won the house competition for not changing out of his jeans. PJ and I dropped out at four and five weeks respectively, but Milo, who liked the feel of rotting denim – 'It's like a second skin!' – was pronounced the champion at ten weeks and told to have a bath or leave.

It was an all-male house.

A house where I claimed as my own a gorilla pube I found on the soap in the shower. Must have been at least thirteen inches long. The guys were impressed but insisted they could do better so we nailed a board to the wall and mounted our curlies for a couple of weeks. I seem to recall this as a time when even fewer women than usual graced our happy home. We were deeply into the 'men without

Pete

One day someone in our house used the washing-up brush to clean the toilet and then put it back in the sink. We found out about it six months later - we thought it was gross but as the brush had been through the sink about two hundred times since then, we didn't figure there was much we could do. Not Mick however, he went and bought a whole new dinner setting and cutlery as well and never ate off any of the house crockery again.

babes' thing, which is a terrible thing. Maybe the worst. It's like living on the Planet of the Dogs without leashes or rolled-up newspapers, a sanction-free zone, where you can go deep and really find your own hostile imbalances. You can see it fully realised in redneck wonderlands like Townsville, where PJ came from. He loved to get drunk and curse off that place. An abbatoir town with a really bad vibe, a masculine vibe. A lot of death and sadness. They kill a lot of beasts up there. Some mornings you can hear the low moaning of the cattle before they're taken up into the food chain. I can strip it back now, see a thematic unity there, a ripeness of the male spirit, like time in the wilderness or the smell of raw pollen. The strong will consume the weak and they won't bother cleaning up after themselves. The thing about guys, the only thing really, is that guys just don't care. It's our little secret. Ask any girl who's ever lived with a herd of us. We'll never wash up, we fart in polite company, and there is absolutely no point in dumping your problems on us because all we want is a regular feeding time and someone to play with. (Want another secret? There isn't a guy alive who hasn't at least tried to lick his own balls.) And just as with a dog pack the truly serious rivalry was reserved for mating season.

PJ and I met her at a B&S Ball. To be fair, he beat me to her. I spied him putting the moves on two girls in the dark recesses of the lobby and decided to ruin his chances. It was a little game we played, popping up at each other's elbow at the worst possible moment to raise the subject of girlfriends, boyfriends, AIDS tests, whatever. But when I cut in, I found one of these girls was a stunning Italian babe with thick dark hair, white skin, eyes you could drown in. A woman to inspire murder. PJ and I circled each other like caged wolves all night.

PJ asked me what I thought of the Italian girl over chocolate milk and cheeseburgers at the traditional post-ball Hungry Jacks breakfast. I said I loved her. He said I loved the girl he was going to marry. A coyote howled somewhere in the distance. We turned one of the paper puzzle mats upside down and drew up the rules of engagement. Total sharing of intelligence. No holding back. No lying. No back stabbing. No chicanery. Guy who gets the first date gets a clear run. The loser retires from the field and runs around the house three times with his underpants on his head. No problemo.

I signed off on this program and immediately set about cheating. My younger brother had helped organise the Ball and possessed the only ticket list, which I quickly obtained and destroyed after a quick scan for Mediterranean female names. PJ and I had both been so drunk we had no idea who we were hunting, but when I saw 'Sophia Gennaro' on the list, it all came flooding back to me. I found her home number in the white pages but her mother answered. After twenty-five minutes of cross-cultural diplomacy I found out that Sophia had gone to

Milo

One morning I heard yelling at the door and
dragged myself out of bed. By the time I got to
the front door you were closing it and standing
there in your dirty stained Y-fronts. Nothing else.
You hadn't shaved for three or four days. Your
hair was everywhere, you hadn't had it cut for
months. These Mormons knocked long enough to
disturb your sleep but you didn't bother to put
anything else on. And you'd sent them on their way
with a prolonged blast of unChristian language.
It's one of the great disappointments of my life
I didn't get up in time to see their faces.
JB: I don't remember that.

work. When this happened three or four times I started to
panic. I knew PJ would have his finders out in the field.

In fact, he came at me two days later and asked flatly
if I had Sophia's phone number. I lied, said no. He smiled.
'Well I guess I win mate because I got her number and I
called her up and I sent her a dozen roses and we're going
on a date this Friday.' I kicked the cat twelve, maybe
thirteen feet across the room when he left. Went into a
black funk for two days. Friday afternoon, I couldn't take

it anymore. I borrowed twenty dollars off Milo and trundled off to the pub to mooch about in the Happy Hour. When I got to the bar, PJ was sitting there, and my heart contracted. I was thinking She had to be there but the joint was empty and I went over and fronted him. 'What's the problem,' I asked. 'What happened to the big date?' He looked at me blankly for a second. 'Oh right. Sorry, JB. That was just bullshit to throw you off. I only spoke to her today. She's got an Italian boyfriend. Mario.' He rolled the name 'Mario' out around a mouthful of cheap scotch and party ice. There was nothing for it but to get pissed together and bitch about poofters. I only saw Sophia once again after that. Sprawled over the bonnet of a Jaguar wearing a sash which read Miss Motor Show.

Shortly afterwards, PJ got engaged at the student Rec Club and moved out. He stood on the bar to make the announcement and, since he was up there, flopped out his chopper for everyone to admire. We had a succession of dud flatmates through PJ's old room. First up, we had the closeted, colour-blind, seven foot male nurse who'd eat a kilo of chips and Twisties while dinner was cooking. He'd have a few bites of Milo's Home Brand meat pie and throw the rest away. But if you didn't cook he'd get shitty. We replaced him with a council worker called Ray who lived on lentils and boiled offal and shed his hair in huge, fist-sized clumps. He built model tanks and little soldiers. He was a fool for the things, would spend months painting each little figure. Visitors would be introduced to his little men before being treated to the matted clots of his hair in the sanitary areas. Ray made way for Malcolm, who couldn't get it together to rinse the sugary bran crap out of his personal set of Charlie Brown breakfast bowls. God, that really bugged me for some reason. Don't know why. I tried everything – returning the bowls to the cupboard unwashed, leaving them in his bed under the doona – he moved on after I brainsnapped and smashed one on the road in front of the house.

The next freak in this carnival side show was Victor the Rasta. I have no idea what possessed us to take him in, some misguided liberal sympathies most likely. Victor liked to carry these big joints of meat round the house, ripping the flesh from the bone with his teeth and leaning into visitors' faces with gobbets of ham trailing out of his mouth. He had no respect for the already tenuous grip of our all-male household on domestic order and hygiene. You'd wake up in the morning to find the house littered with empty pizza trays, old spare ribs, chicken carcasses, beer bottles and salami rind. You could clean them away, but they'd be back the next morning. He'd play the stereo all night and bring friends around for nitrous oxide binges. They were dentists. They once bought a tank of the stuff, figuring that at a hundred bucks for the tank and fifty for a refill it was a bargain. They got this thing at midday and had sucked it dry by four o'clock. They'd fight over who got the hose, punching each other to get at it then sucking on the tube till they passed out. Now don't get me wrong, I'll get into a binge as quickly as the next man, but there is such a thing as dignity. And flaking out under a blanket of old pizza boxes isn't even close.

After tossing Victor out and passing his details on to Immigration, we interviewed an angry woman, who fled upon finding the Champion Pube Board hidden behind the shower curtain, a Haitian girl on the run from a mad flatmate – she kept her used toilet paper in a bucket. Said the sewer people wanted it to control her thoughts – and a muscular Christian, who assured us that knuckle push-ups were an excellent way of avoiding temptation.

We still thought of the empty room as PJ's at this

point. Nobody had stayed long enough, or lodged in our affections firmly enough to displace him as its spiritual owner. Share house veterans will be familiar with this, but the rest of you can think of it as the Dead Beagle Syndrome – the tendency for subsequent pets to suffer in comparison with the original and best. Outstanding flatmates can place a spiritual lock on a bedroom for up to a year after everyone who knew them has moved out.

'Oh I don't know about putting your Liberty print chair in there. That used to be Damien's room … No, I never met him but … you know … he dabbled in the black arts.'

We finally offered PJ's room to McGann, a travelling American in his mid-forties. He was one of the fittest men I've ever lived with, in much better shape than Milo and I, who were at least twenty years his junior. He canoed three hundred miles every week. We wondered what possible excuse he had at his age for living with the likes of us. I took him for one of those guys you meet in share housing, one of those guys who's a bit older, done far too many drugs, very untrustworthy, kind of dangerous around naive young women, able to project a certain mystique and play within his limitations, the ageing rock star of the share house circuit. He claimed to be on the run from a bad divorce in the US. Said he'd come to Australia to complete his education while doing some travel. His story moved about a bit under fire. Some days he'd be studying English Lit, on others a PhD in American History. He was studying something and getting all sort of grants for it, but you could never pin him down on the details. Suspicious? We thought so. But who cares? It was plausible, we'd had enough interviewing for one year, so we took him on spec. We wanted the bills paid. McGann wanted a place that was 'cool', and didn't come with any 'hassles'. He hinted that his last house had been very 'uncool' and the flatmates were very fond of 'hassling' him. We shrugged, not realising that he was coding a message for us. If you're seriously looking at doing the share housing thing, you've got to learn to decipher the codes. In Sydney for instance, a 'broad-minded' house is either gay or gay friendly. In Brisbane, houses located in 'green, leafy suburbs' will have a bucket bong pretty much continually fired up in the living room. For McGann, a cool house with no hassles was one that didn't look sideways at his huge appetite for commercial sex, and didn't mention it around his fat girlfriend, Amanda.

McGann had done the figures at the end of a twelve month period when he'd had no sex at all. He went out on a lot of dates, bought a lot of dinners and flowers, sat through plays and gallery openings, expressed his feelings, told all the right lies, but at the end of the year, there'd been no action down south. After the final unsuccessful date went home in a taxi, he sat down and worked out that he'd spent $4300 on these women. He caught a cab into the red light district, walked into a brothel, pulled out $120 and a girl had sex with him. From that moment on, he was a convert. A believer.

What did we care? As long as people pay the rent and stay out of your room, you can't be too sniffy about their private lives. We'd come home every now and then, there'd be a strange car parked in front of the house and the driver would nod to us as we walked in. Letting us know he was there. Ten, fifteen minutes later, a woman would emerge from McGann's room and pick her way through the piles of sports equipment blocking our hallway. Later, McGann would emerge in his sarong, looking very relaxed. That was kind of horrible actually – the idea that he'd just been having sex and now he was wearing this loose sarong, his wet wedding tackle liable to spill out at any moment – but otherwise, we didn't care. We'd have a drink with the drivers on hot afternoons, invite them in to watch the cricket. Sometimes if McGann finished early, we'd fix the girl and her pimp a cup of tea and some biscuits. We didn't want the girl to assume we thought any less of her for having sex with our flatmate.

A few months after McGann had settled in, we hosted a party for some babes who were taking off on a round-the-world trip to avoid looming career decisions. Things went downhill fast after the ceremonial spearing of the keg in the back yard. As it got dark, my furniture went into the maw of a huge burning pit beside the Hills Hoist.

We had excavated this thing as a barbecue. The furniture was Milo's decision alone. He wasn't into the share house consultancy thing. People were cold, so in went the brown couch. I was kind of down on him for that, but he forgot to remove his stash from one of the cushions, so it evened out. The way these things always seem to.

Milo and I sat in the living room later that night, surrounded by the debris, sunburned and hopelessly drunk, knowing in our hearts that we would not clean up for at least three months. McGann, however, was bouncing off the walls. A long day of drinking with pneumatic

Terry

A bunch of us were at King Street one night. There was a plate of green stuff festering on the coffee table. It may have been bacon at one time - but that's just a guess, nobody could really tell. Sandra made her usual remarks about 'you boys' living in a pigsty. She had asked for a cup of coffee but been made a bowl of one because of the clean cup shortage. Meanwhile, I was sitting in the single lounge chair. I let my left hand drop onto the carpet looking for my beer but fumbled upon something I thought was a shoelace. When I picked it up to have a closer look at it I realised it was the major portion of a rat's tail.

wonderbabes had touched off some elemental drive within him, jacked his soul into some giant black generator and cranked it up to critical mass. He was raving about his student grant, $6000 which had just gone into his account. We found him on the phone working his way through the Yellow Pages. E for Escort. We started ringing them back, cancelling orders. But we weren't dealing with drunken bravado here, we had a case of rutting madness in the house. While Milo and I consulted in the kitchen, McGann tried to place an order for a dozen Asian girls and a gram of speed from some dodgey escort agency. We could see him getting bilked out of every cent he had. The house did not need the hassle. It would very definitely not be *cool*. We cancelled the girls and put the soothers on McGann by telling him he could take us to a strip club for a drink, and if there were any hookers about, we'd sit around and watch him get laid. But he'd be paying for everything. We stressed that, shouted it at him as he called us a taxi. Milo had five bucks to his name and I had $1.38 in phone jar change. We planned to drive McGann into town, get him so drunk he passed out, or in the final extreme, knock him unconscious. Total cost: about $150, all down to him.

We cabbed it to the Valley, to this pre-Fitzgerald strip club which had a brothel attached to it. Risky, but we had to string him along. Two hours later, McGann was still conscious and a big whack of his student grant had been poured down our throats in the form of tequila laybacks administered by topless barmaids. Our table had become the centre of attention, the terminal point for an unceasing stream of bouncers, hookers and waitresses. There was shouting and singing and the sound of smashing glass. At other tables, businessmen hunkered down sullenly over their drinks. A well-known Marxist university lecturer, a politically correct hatchet man who'd been trapped at his table when we came in, tried to sneak out during a round of laybacks. Milo spotted him and started a commotion, scrambling towards the guy with a cigarette lighter, mumbling something about marking him 'as of the Beast.' McGann chose that exact moment to make his move on The Fabulous Tina. He launched himself from a paralytic stupor into full flight across the top of our table, sending beer bottles and shot glasses everywhere as he dived. He didn't make it, drastically misjudging the distance and his ability to take it in a blur of fluid action. His chin hit the stage and he managed to get out a scream before the bouncers descended for the last time and threw us out.

We were hoping that McGann might have folded by this stage, but he picked himself up from the footpath and said this was the best night he'd had in ages. That black wave of despair, unknown outside the desperate wee hours, swept down on me. We tried to get into an illegal casino, where the alcohol is free as long as you're losing – the economics seem feasible when you're drunk – but they wouldn't have us because we weren't wearing ties. The casino people referred us to an address up the street, a white stucco palace with a lot of friendly women hanging out of the windows. We thundered up the stairs, ran past the receptionist and settled in at the bar. Two hours later, the bar was dry and nobody had made any bookings. Men in tuxedos began to block the exits. Our plan was falling to pieces. We had to throw McGann to them or they would have executed us out on the footpath. I woke up on the floor next to Milo with the sun slanting in on me, mouth like a dry turd and heavy peak-hour traffic roaring by outside. McGann had taken four girls, spent all of his grant, lifted Milo's Bankcard and whacked another grand's worth of whoopee on the plastic before the sun came up.

McGann left a few weeks later. He didn't have any trouble paying Milo back. Got the money to him within a couple of days. But like I said, we never really got round to cleaning up after that party. The disorder which had been lurking at the edge of things took dominion and McGann couldn't handle it. As the piles of dishes and scraps of food took root in the kitchen, the KFC and Hungry Jacks flotsam which had been quiescent since Victor the Rasta's departure reappeared through the house. Most of the containers were empty, crumpled and spent, but here and there, a half eaten Whopper or Chicken Speciality perched on the arm of a chair, slowly melting and growing into the fabric. Beer cans and stubbies sprouted from within the shifting dunes of discarded junk food artefacts – only one or two to begin with, establishing a tentative hold, testing the atmosphere, then erupting in fantastic promiscuous discharges of lagers and ales and dark malty stouts, torn cardboard cartons and unknowable numbers of plastic six pack rings. Porn mags, junk mail, newspapers, sports supplements, comic books, text books, lecture notes, tissues, paper plates, napkins, pizza boxes, plastic bags, pie tins, flavoured milks, tee shirts, socks and rotting vegetable matter were churned, shredded, ground down, chewed up, digested, crushed, pulped, torpedoed, bombed, burned and eviscerated into layers and hillocks of generic land fill. We chose to ignore the sounds of rummaging rats and skittering roaches, to cope with the blue-green algal bloom spreading out of the kitchen sink and to shrug when the black oily toxins began leaking from the vegetable crisper. However, the trails of fat white maggots, headed from the kitchen to our bedrooms like ships of the line, brought a response. Milo and I bought a couple of silly hats, some high-powered water pistols, filled them with kerosene and went hunting. McGann, on the other hand, had been cooking in the back yard for a week, heating Milo's Army Reserve surplus ration packs over the fire pit by the Hills Hoist. When he finished the last of those and was faced with coming down to our level – sucking the jelly directly out of the green tubes of army jam for sustenance – he moved out.

'I just can't stand it,' he said.

With the house in such a state, the only replacement we could get was my friend Taylor, the taxi driver. He was coming out of a doomed relationship with a bikie chick and was knocking back two or three bottles of overproof rum every day. There were some dark forces at work inside him, manifesting themselves in the black Special Forces tee shirt, jungle camouflage pants and white running shoes which he never took off. We told people the white running shoes were the last vestiges of his human personality trying to hang on. When they were replaced by army boots it would be random sniper time.

Taylor was usually out of his tree by mid-morning. By lunch time he'd be

Des

We had a cleaning lady. Gail. A western suburbs middle-aged cleaning lady with a shrieking voice. She'd start the morning with a bourbon and coke at our place. She'd come in and clean around us in our bedrooms, even when we had someone in there. The dishes piled up once when she was away. It got so bad in the end that we just dumped the whole thing in the bathtub and filled that up. But then we left it for a week. The water was just rancid. Lucky John got pissed one night, we heard all this splashing and crashing and clashing in the bathroom. We ran in there and he'd gotten naked, crawled in with the dishes and the toxic water.

Milo

I remember that we all chose to ignore the life
forms growing in the carpet, and to ignore the
food and rotting matter in the fridge and the
oven. We watched the knives and forks grow mould,
and watched the garden grow up over the Hills
Hoist. It was the maggots which finally got us to
move. I don't remember how long I spent on the
cleaning frenzy. I didn't know where to start. I
thought I could start at the edges and chip away
to the heart. Then I thought fuck it if I drive a
stake through the heart it'll die and wither. I
alternated between the two, but nothing seemed to
work, bagging and vacuuming methodically inwards,
or just diving into the middle with a shovel and
tossing it all out the windows. Days went by and
days started and finished without any difference
except that I was losing weight. We were doing it
to get the bond back but in hindsight I should
have just accepted the money wasn't worth it and
moved out.

unbearable, crashing around the house, headbutting the
fridge, roaring like a bull elk. He was very much the man
in pain. I'd lock myself in my room, but he'd pound on the
door, demanding to be let in for a drink. Most days, he'd
give up after five minutes, but on one occasion he was

determined enough to climb onto the roof and rappel down through my bedroom window with a bottle of Brandavino stuck in his web belt. He plopped on the floor, legs splayed out in front on him and started drinking and talking as though this was the most normal thing in the world. He later ambushed us on the way back from a paddlepop expedition. We'd gone looking to see if he wanted any, but couldn't find him. When we came back he attacked us with a plastic pistol. Must have been hiding for three quarters of an hour. Told us if the pistol had been real we'd be dead.

Time to move on.

Which meant cleaning up to reclaim the bond. We set aside two weeks for the job, but I got some temp work in a typing pool and Taylor just disappeared. Milo ended up doing most of the work. I'd come home at night and the poor bastard would have this drawn look around his eyes. He'd have been at it for eight hours straight, but you couldn't see a damn bit of difference. He gave up after a week. I had to finish the job. I was on the case, when my friend Tim reappeared after a year in Asia. He'd been imprisoned in a Hong Kong asylum after a vodka binge. Woke up strapped to a bed in this enormous nut house surrounded by about seven thousand Chinese mental patients. The doctors had him full of lithium for the first week because he kept trying to escape. When he calmed down, they let him wander around, pretty much unsupervised. He got a phone call through to a friend in

Canberra, also called Tim, who worked for Defence Intelligence. Tim Number Two flew straight up to Hong Kong and blustered his way into the hospital, putting the frighteners on the staff with his Australian security passes. He busted Tim out of there and they fled the colony with the law on their tails. The other Tim dropped my friend Tim off in Brisbane, and he made his way to my house at one in the morning.

I was sitting up, pulling cones, watching some woeful sitcom on the teev when he came through the door. I didn't recognise him straight off – he was cadaverous and looked authentically mad. But I eventually worked it out and told him to crash in my room. I looked after him for three days. When he wasn't comatose on Valium, he was setting little fires in the kitchen. Eventually I waited until he passed out, ran around the house collecting my stuff, and split. I closed the door and left him in there on the carpet. He must have been okay because I moved in with him and some other guys a week later.

MONEY

THE NERVE TONIC
THAT GETS AT THE
CAUSE OF YOUR
TROUBLE

Evan

ON THE INFAMOUS
FRIDGE PISSING INCIDENT

After the frypan, the fridge is the greatest source of angst and disruption in any share house. Everybody complains but nobody is willing to do the minimum necessary to stop it from toxing out.

My friend Evan tells me he had a flat-mate who bought a whole bunch of those magnetic fridge letters for leaving notes to the house. Stuff like 'Hey guys. Let's clean up'. But the house just rearranged them to say things like 'Say no to anal flatmates.'

God knows what sort of message Evan could have spelled out with the magnet-ic fridge letters if the following incident had taken place in that house.

EVAN LIVES BY HIMSELF NOWADAYS.

I awoke fully clothed on the brown couch in our lounge room with only hazy memories of the night before. I'd been out drinking, really heavy drinking - two fisted, round-the-clock, saturation-point binge-drinking - and I had the uncomfortable feeling that I'd pissed in the fridge on coming home. I had no conscious memory of having done it, but this little voice in the back of my mind kept whispering. 'You know you pissed in the fridge don't you? I stumbled out to the kitchen but I couldn't see any evidence, only the remains of some kippers plastered on the walls. The issue rested until a few days later when Fran, my housemate, came into my room with a disturbed look on her face.

'Hey, did you know the fridge is having some defrosting trouble?' she asked.

'Really?' I said, idly turning the pages of the book I was reading.

'Yeah,' she said. 'It's got two inches of water in the veggie tray.'

Coffee sprayed from my mouth.

'Aaahh, I'd better have a look at that,' I said, and followed her to the kitchen. I pottered around the fridge while she sliced the veggies she'd taken out of the crisper. My mind was racing.

'Probably the thermostat or something -
seems to be all right now.' I said. I was
stalling for time. I needed to instigate a
full forensic search of the driptray without arousing suspicion. Trouble was, she was
already hunkered down at the chopping
board, slicing and dicing the possibly con-
taminated carrots and brussel sprouts.
'Uhm, Fran, you're not planning to eat
those veggies are you?' I asked.
'Yeah,' she replied. 'What else would I do
with them?'
'Well I really don't think you ought to,' I
said, desperately casting about for some
excuse, some gambit to send her out of the
room for a few minutes while I cleaned up
in her absence.
'Why not?' she asked.
'Well the fridge water, it's not healthy,'
I said.
She wanted to know what was wrong with it.
I could see there was nothing for it but to
come clean.
'It's like this,' I said. 'There's been a
little accident. Adrian got really pissed
and ... ahm anyway, he told me he thinks he
might have urinated in the fridge ...'
'What!!!'
'Exactly, terrible accident, but the thing
is, I think he's very embarrassed about it

so I wouldn't mention it, OK?' I blathered
and improvised but it didn't really seem as
if it was going to be OK. I bolted when
Fran stormed into Adrian's room and started
yelling at him.
It was horrible.
I sent them my rent and two weeks notice
the next day and never went back.

THE SMALL WORLD
EXPERIENCE

The thing about Brisbane is that everyone knows you or knows about you. In small world theory, there's only six points of separation between any two individuals, but you can trim down the numbers in Brisbane. Everyone's stories intersect, crossing over and through each other like sticky strands of destiny and DNA. I lived with a dozen people in one house, and none of them were formally interviewed before they moved in. That's not unusual. You tend to rent whole houses with friends and the friends of friends in

Hack

My friend Claudia and this other girl wanted to get a guy in to their house to do the guy stuff. Change the light bulbs, beat up the burglars and so on. They took this guy after interviewing about fifteen others. He was cool. Been there a week, the guy stuff's getting done, they're all getting along. They're sitting in the lounge room one night with the dog, watching a movie. Half way through this guy reaches over and starts wanking off the dog. Claudia freaked and said, 'What are you doing? That's disgusting! Stop it right now!' He turned to her and looked at her really carefully and said, 'Just helping out a mate.'

Brisbane. Even moving into a room in an existing household is mostly a matter of trading history and establishing common reference points. 'Oh right. You know Chris. He used to live with my last flatmate's girlfriend and her cousin.' Then Chris, the girlfriend and her cousin turn up to help you move your furniture in, and you all sit on the front verandah drinking tea, watching the storms roll in and pushing back the envelope of the extended family that is Brisbane.

We even had a generational thing going at Duke Street, one of the most frightening houses I have ever lived in. My uncle Robbie, a former hippy, turns up with a parental relief parcel one day and tells me he lived in the exact same house twenty years ago as a professional desperado in the early 1970s.

The place was in better condition in those days. The owners rented out single rooms rather than the whole house. Robbie and three friends went along thinking they were getting the whole deal, but there were two guys in the front room who came with the house, these two fugitives from Western Australia. Nobody knew who they were. The hippies said, 'Who the hell are you?' and the guys said, 'We live here.' The landlord had rented the room to a couple of outlaws. One was Ron and the other was Max. Max was wanted in Western Australia, South Australia and Victoria. Ron was running from Western Australia, the Northern Territory and Tasmania. They'd made their way to Brisbane, changing their last names as they went but sticking with their christian names to avoid confusion. They were okay. Some Orange People moved into the neighbourhood and someone stupidly invited one of them around for a feed. This Orange person turned up with another five or six Orange people, and they just wouldn't leave. Set up camp in the living room. Started eyeing off the chicks. It looked ugly for a while, until Ron and Max returned from some job they'd pulled, beat the shit out of the Orange People and threw them out into the street.

Duke Street's standards had slipped in the

intervening years. There were about ten of us living there. Another house full of fuck-offs and misfits and perennial students. We had neighbours on all sides. Complaining neighbours. They hassled us constantly. So constantly in fact that we kept a Complaint Scoreboard on the fridge door. When we got to ten complaints, we'd have a party. You'd think they'd learn, but they never did. The morning after the party, they'd give us a head start on the next one with a fresh round of complaints. We were all living off welfare at this time, and the DSS had the place on the area map, flagged with a skull and crossbones. Dole fascists regularly descended upon the place in human waves. They'd given up trying to pick us off individually – the house was so disorganised that even at six in the morning their chances of catching the right person at home were less than zero. So they sent a couple of blanket sweeps through the place, kicked down the door at five in the morning, sprayed capsicum gas in our eyes and beat us on the soles of our feet with big sticks, said we were all being reviewed and the whole house would have to attend a compulsory seminar. It was a horrible joke. A fat Christian told us to keep our spirits up, showed us a motivational video and made us tell each other we were valuable human beings. Magyver got caught trying to make off with the powdered coffee.

Magyver had the room next to me. He only ever wore blue nylon Dunlop overalls and although he was a qualified psycho-therapist, he worked on a mushroom farm and seemed at home there. He was only employed part-time, but he enjoyed shovelling shit and carting trays of mushrooms about so much that he spent all of his spare time out there too. Really got into it. Last I heard, he'd gone to South America, looking for the Surinam toad, which someone told him has a small concave depression in its back – 'I'm telling you, man. It's a freak show!' – and while he was over there checking it out he met some Chilean girl in a brothel. She wasn't a hooker – just had

Susan

I once sublet my room to an old woman for three months. When I got back from travelling my flatmates told me she belonged to some weird religious cult. She used to wander around the house at night, holding candles, waiting for fellow cult members to come and stare in through the windows.

a room on the top floor. Magyver shacked up with her in this cat house. He sent back one postcard, said she was the most fantastic woman he'd ever known. When his visa ran out, he gave her three thousand dollars to arrange a passage back to Australia, but the next thing he knew, she had a job with the World Bank. That was the last he ever heard of her.

Neal the albino moontanner had the master bedroom in the house. You'd come home at one or two in the morning and he'd be in his underpants, stretched out on the banana lounge in the front yard, staring up at the heavens.

'What's happening Neal?'

'Moontanning, man.'

One night he came in all shaken up. He'd been checking out the girls across the road from us, whom he was kind of keen on. Not looking eager, just kicking back on the banana lounge. They were cute, in a cashmere sweater kind of way, and Neal was certain that if they could just be introduced to sex by an albino moontanner, they'd never look back. Sadly one of the girls spilled out of a cab, drunk, with a flat-headed rugby type who fucked her like a dog on the front lawn in the moonlight. Took a few cones before Neal could get over that one.

After catching those moonrays, Neal liked sleeping more than anything else. Had this theory about it. The hassle avoidance theory of sleep – 'I'd sleep twenty hours to avoid a hassle,' he'd say. He had a rumpled street-dwelling demeanour and his room

Bob

These girls I knew, lived just around the corner, got this guy in. He'd been there for three or four days, everything was fine. But they came home one night and found him on the couch with all the lights on, completely naked, sucking on their panties. He booked himself into the loony bin the next day.

looked like the inside of a big St. Vinnies clothing bin. There was no mattress to speak of, just enough rags and old clothes to pile up and crawl under so that it didn't matter. His best friend was Howie, a mad red-headed bastard who became a virtual flatmate by reason of his never leaving the house for more than a few hours at a time. When he did leave, it was only to pick up one of the rusting, arthritic old British motorcycles he and Neal used to strip down in the spare living room, the one in which we normally played basketball. They'd only ever get half way through the job, and then the bike would be gone, replaced by another in even worse condition.

Neal and Howie were guys with way too much time on their hands. I was back doing Law by this time, but I gave up studying at the house because of the noise. Noise from the indoor golf driving range, noise from the motorbike corridor time trials, noise from the chainsaw Howie attached to his arm while they role-played *Evil Dead* and *Evil Dead 2*. He loved strapping on that big Makita and charging around, looking for Undead zombies to chop up. His eyes were strangely vacant as he laughed and smote the fibro walls, tearing chunks out of them in roaring clouds of asbestos dust. At least with the chainsaw you'd hear him coming. Golf practice was way past frightening. Neal and Howie didn't fuck around with office Putt Putt. They teed up at the end of the hall and smashed these drives away with full blooded swings of their woods and

five irons. The walls left standing after the chainsaw
massacre were pock marked by the sort of holes that
machine guns leave in the Bugs Bunny cartoons.

Satomi Tiger was the first foreign person I lived
with. She was only with us for a short time. Disappeared as
mysteriously as she came.

'I go now.'

Harry

I got bitten but not by one of my flatmates. It was
the man who lived in the room underneath my
girlfriend's house. His name was Rick and he was
shacked up with a girl called Mary. He'd get pissed and
beat up on her all the time. One time Mary got so beat
up that she crawled outside and hid under his Pulsar.
Rick was so drunk he was smashing everything in the
house screaming, 'Mary Mary.' He came upstairs while we
were watching the TV, me and the two girls who lived
there. My girlfriend said to me, 'You're the only man
in the house, deal with this.' So I said 'Rick,' big
pause, 'fuck off'. And he attacked me. At first I
pushed him over. But he got up. I pushed him over again
and he got up. I hit him hard and he got up. I hit him
really hard and he got up. I hit him with all my
strength and smashed his face in to the point where
his face was a bloody mess, and he got up. And suddenly
I realised that this was the man who would not die.

But it was interesting having her there. She freaked out one day, because a neighbour came to the window to ask for a kiss. God knows what she made of the chainsaw man. Some cops dragged her home once after they'd caught her riding a scooter through the city, unlicensed, doing 90 in a 60 zone the wrong way up a one-way street. They nearly shot out her tires before she stopped. They were

It was frightening. He should have been completely fucked, but he got up. When I hit him with everything I had and he got up, I felt the Fear. Then he bit me on the chest through my favourite green-striped shirt, bit me just under my nipple. Now I'm really funny about my nips. I've never liked girls slurping on them or anything. He took a chunk out of my chest, a big fucking bite, destroyed my favourite green-striped shirt. At this point my girlfriend phoned a guy up the road who was a football player. She couldn't call the police because of all the drugs in the house. The footy player burst in as we're fighting, grabbed his mate, the guy who was biting my chest, and pushed him through a wall. He's going, 'Calm down man.' And the guy's going, 'I wanna kill him.' Now I've got this perfect set of teeth marks just below my nipple.

furious and yelled at her until they realised she didn't understand a word they were saying. Then they spoke very slowly and used lots of hand puppet gestures to explain that she could not do what she was doing. Satomi Tiger bowed and smiled some more.

'Domo arrigato. Domo. Domo.'

Then she hops on the bike and blasts off in the same direction. 0 to 90 in three seconds. They ran her down again, brought her home and tore Neal a new arsehole for letting her ride his bike.

We liked Satomi Tiger's quiet, rent-paying ways, so we ran a succession of foreign students through her old sleepout after she disappeared. It was a very small, naked room, the worst in the place. A major train line ran parallel with that side of the house, so none of us would bed down there, but it was perfect for clueless, rent-paying foreigners.

First we had Patrick, the boy from Hong Kong. He lasted a day, and spent that day in front of the mirror in his underpants grooming his hair. Loved that hair. He got it right and moved out. We had some Baptist black guy from Africa, a bible-bashing footwasher but he was okay. Really took to the basketball court. Then he took to the hallucinogenic fungus in the back yard and that was the end of him. Finally there came Krishna, an easily titillated Malay Indian guy. Loved the SBS Friday night porn. The merest flash of nipple would send him off like a retarded child on a nitrous binge. He was thirty-five. Whenever we

Jed

We got bored a lot. There were about six of us
home one night, in this big old house with a fireplace, very bored, watching teev, nothing on.
Someone tossed a match into the fireplace.
Somebody else tossed a cigarette after it. Then
somebody spat in there. Someone picked up a glass
and threw it in. Then an iron went in. Then this
frenzy took hold for about five minutes, everything
went in there. Arms were being ripped off chairs,
books, plates, random furniture. Then somebody made
a move for the TV and we came back to earth, wres-
tled him away from it, then shrugged and threw him
in too. I don't know why that happened.

passed the bong around Krishna felt duty-bound to point
out that in Malaysia old Mahatir would have you swinging
by your heels for this sort of thing. Neal finally convinced
him to pull a cone for multiculturalism. He took a few
smokes, started giggling and fled to his room. He legged it
the following day. After Krishna, we decided it was all just
too hard. The house voted to take a rent rise and let the
sleepout lie fallow. Not surprising really. I've always tried to
do the right thing by our multicultural brethren, but it just
never seems work out. Like with this Chinese Chef who
moved into another place I lived once. I came back from a

road trip to find this Chinese guy had moved in. Someone said he liked cooking.

'A Chinese chef,' I said. 'Outstanding.'

They could have been more specific. He liked to cook fried rice in a wok on a gas burner beside his chair in the lounge as he sat watching television. After a few weeks, the lino acquired a sticky, sooty complexion from the soy sauce and the TV screen was flecked with burned rice. He'd made a special deal with the fruit shop where he bought in bulk at discount rates and he was always dragging these 250kg sacks of potatoes or carrots up the back steps. Four weeks later, we had to sneak the soggy residue into a nearby industrial bin because the neighbours were coming over to complain about the smell. The same thing happened with the cabbages a month after that. We were working up the nerve to kick the Chinese chef out when by a strange twist of events he threw us out. He brought his mother over from China for a visit, had her staying in his room. The Chinese chef couldn't admit to the filthy mess he was leaving around him – the kitchen was about an inch deep in chicken bones and cabbage leaves by this stage – so he blamed us. His mother stewed on it for a few days, then got the real estate heavies to turf us out.

Satomi Tiger's neighbour in the bad side of the house was Jabba the Hutt. He was enrolled in civil engineering at Queensland Uni, but as far as I know, he never made it to class. Not once. Sat round all day watching

TV. Even on golf days. He'd watch the kids' shows in the morning. Then the soapies through the day. Then the news. Then the evening shows. Then the late night movies, the dire sitcoms and those obscure, undead fillers like *Mod Squad* and Chuck Connor's *Thrillseekers*. *The thrillseeker,* said Chuck. *A special breed of cat.* And finally Jabba would stack some zzz's, get up the next day and start all over again. Day after day. Week after week. For months without a break. Then one Saturday night, completely out of character, he got so drunk he wet himself. We threw him out the back yard, turned the hose on him. He stayed out there all night. I got up the next morning and there he was, cleaned up, lying in front of the teev again.

Across the hall from Jabba lived Mick, our racist in residence. Mick blew into town from Perth and knew someone who knew someone at the house. Nobody will fess up to it now, so I guess that link is going to have to stay lost. We should have known really. He didn't like chilli, didn't like curry, didn't like anything Asian. Had these very strange views on Asia and food. We threw a party to introduce him to Brisbane, but he was comatose in a corner by nine o'clock. Completely pissed. Vomiting and sucking air through the mess with a thick, obscene snorkelling sound. Every so often he'd claw his way up, shuffle round and stare at you, nose to nose. It was very weird. After that party, he awoke in the dark screaming abuse at some imaginary old guy he saw at the foot of his bed. Said it was the guy on the

Mandy

I was hanging around Martin's house over Christmas. There were heaps of guys hanging there too. They were getting into not wearing shirts. Then they started writing words on their chests. Slug. Loser. But that wasn't cool enough so they started cutting it into themselves with razor blades. Then they were sticking pieces of broken mirror onto their bodies with glue.

cover of The Cure album. *Standing On A Beach*.

'Freak show!' said Magyver.

Mick's neighbour's were Colin and Stepan, a pre-realised Xerox of Beavis and Butthead. Their rooms formed an L-shape around two sides of the lounge, but they had so much in common it suited them to kick out the fibro-slab divider and hang a curtain between their respective domains. They were friends of Neal's and were attracted to Duke Street by the minimal rent and crack house ambience. They gave our bucket bong such a workout that if you somehow ingested the water you'd die. You'd have been the first reported dope casualty in history. There was a different type of smell around their part of the house. That was Stepan. He ate so much speed his body ran at white heat nine days out of ten and exuded a really foul, sour sort of amphetamine sweat. His thesis supervisor refused to see him unless he bathed immediately before their meetings.

Colin, with two failed attempts at adult education behind him, was trying to work up some enthusiasm for the world of employment. Seeing as Stepan managed to vacate the house by 9.30 most morning's – to get some quality time in at the campus video game parlour – Colin asked him to be sure and wake him up before leaving, so he could seize the day, get a job and a life. Stepan tried for a week, but he'd come back in the afternoon and Colin would still be getting out of bed. Then he'd abuse Stepan for not getting him up. Finally Stepan closed all of the windows and doors that could be shut, slapped Colin awake, put a lit candle on the floor, and said, 'I've turned on every gas tap in the house. If you're still asleep when the gas reaches this candle, the house is going to blow up and you are going to die. If you just get out of bed and snuff out the candle you are also going to die, because the gas will choke you to death.' The house didn't blow up, Colin slept through the whole thing, and the place smelt of gas for a month. But we were so impressed with Stepan's *Man from UNCLE* ingenuity that we all made a point of rushing into Colin's room each morning and kicking the shit out of him in a bid to make him change his ways. It did. He moved out.

Boredom is a terrible thing in a group like this. When you are living alone, you can get out of the house and deal with it. But when you get a lot of bored people in one place, it gets ugly. You'll wind up putting bananas in your underpants and butt-walking across the lounge room. Or running around the block, naked, with a purple cape flapping behind you, singing *Nananana Nananana Nananana Batman*. It was boredom that drove Howie and Neal to smash the beer bottle pyramid to pieces. An orgiastic riot of boredom-inspired destruction. Magyver and I came home to find the kitchen table splintered to matchwood, the fridge door hanging by one twisted metal hinge and a month's worth of meat patties and Sara Lee Poundcake splattered and smeared over the walls and ceiling. Woolworths had been running specials on both items and Magyver had insisted on buying in bulk for an even bigger discount. The store manager's eyes must have bugged out of his skull when this fool rushed in waving crumpled banknotes in his face and demanding as much of the expired stock as he could carry. All for nothing now of course. Neal was in the lounge room watching *Wheel Of Fortune* and I said, 'Hey Neal. What's happening?'

'Madness,' he shrugged.

There were diversions. We saw the house next door get pulled off its stumps and taken away in the middle of the night. Happens all the time in Brisbane. Old Queenslanders get chopped in two, hauled up onto a flat-bed and driven off to some yuppie's farm. Neal had his own theory about it. *The old house graveyard.* The movers came around and told us when they'd be doing it so everyone in the neighbourhood prepared meals and stayed up way past their bedtime, picnicking in the front garden or gathering in little knots under the lamp posts. It turned into a street festival. Howie offered to help cut the house up. Neal dragged the moontanning lounge out. Mick got drunk and had a sit-down in the back of a police car. Jabba watched

Launz

Boredom gets to be a really great motivator. Kevin and I were bored and decided to set up an interesting photograph. We got him to sit on the toilet and floated a little boat with some smoke mixture in it. The idea was that we'd shoot a sequence of him being enveloped in smoke and the last frame would be the smoke clearing and this hand coming out of the bowl. We had a mannequin hand. The problem with this smoke mixture is that when you burn it you have to make sure it's in a long and thin, or thin and flat state. If you have it in a ball, it doesn't lose heat quickly enough. It moves to this second stage burn which we didn't know about. So Kev is sitting on the toilet, the smoke is coming then there is this almighty flash and Kev is leaping out of the bathroom clutching his flaming arse. That's what boredom will do.

Launz

There was a mouse in Chester Street which lived in
the stove. It liked to come out and dance. We were
getting real tired of this mouse. One night we
were sitting up late, drinking and playing cards.
Kevin said, 'We've got to get rid of this mouse.'
I said 'Okay, how?' Throw things at it. So we
propped up in the kitchen and started throwing
cutlery. We emptied our kitchen drawers trying to
nail the little bastard - knives, forks, egg-beat-
ers and everything. It would go away for three or
four minutes then come back. Finally Kev said,
'I've got a plan.' He wandered over to the stove,
put on all the gas taps, wandered back and sat
down with a box of matches. I asked what he was
doing. He said when the mouse came out he was
going to throw a lighted match at it and blow it
to pieces. I took them off him and went to the
shop for a mouse trap. But all they had was this
huge rat trap and rat traps don't trigger when
little field mice gnaw off the bait. So we filed it
back to a hair trigger. Re-baited it and set it on
the stove. About an hour later we were asleep when
this huge snap came from the kitchen. We found the
trap had got this poor little mouse but it had hit
it so hard that both of its eyeballs had shot out
of its head and bounced across the floor.

television. The guys taking the house were hopeless. They'd get it half way up the steep front yard and it would slip back down again. Their wheels got bogged in the mud they churned up, windows exploded, chains broke and the outside toilet was accidentally destroyed.

When the house disappeared we discovered the girl in the red panties. Our view had been blocked by the old place, but with the line of sight unobscured it wasn't long before somebody spotted her dancing in her kitchen between 5.10 and 5.25 pm every day. She was a dancing fool. Never let us down. It was the only schedule the house stuck to, elbowing and shouldering each other out of the way for the best window seat.

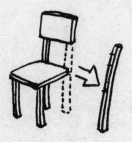

A CHAIR COSTS LESS IF IT'S ALREADY BEEN PAID FOR

I knew my time at Duke Street had passed when I came home and there was this guy lying on the ironing board. Flat on his back. Shivering. I asked Jabba, 'Who the hell's this?' but he just shrugged. 'Been there all day,' and went back to the soaps. I edged over to the guy who suddenly turned his glazed eyes on me. He was on a really weird trip. Said something about being a ship in stormy seas. I couldn't talk sense into him so I threw a blanket across the ironing board. But he freaked out, thought it was a shroud. He started yelling, 'I'm dying. I can feel it. I'm going I'm going!' Screamed that the only thing which could save him was mouth to mouth resuscitation.

I said, 'Sorry pal, you're a dead man.'

Fish Finger

BIG DINNER PARTY THIS WEEKEND?

Or just some friends who've
dropped in unannounced.

Surprise them with a
Fish Finger recipe.

Fondue, Casseroles or Grills.
Nothing impresses like a
Fresh Fish Finger.

EVEN YOU can prepare them like a Pro.
From the casual sophistication of Fish
Finger Kebabs to a six course set-piece
dinner arranged around the magnificent
Fish Fingers in Aspic your guests will
be as surprised as you were on discov-
ering this culinary Must Have.

FISH FINGERS AHOY?

Enjoy!

THE SMALL WORLD
EXPERIENCE

5

THE
FOSTER-LINDBURGH
INCIDENT

The dead man on the ironing board had me rattled so I moved down to Melbourne. Not sure why. When you live in Brisbane, you don't really think about Melbourne. It's a long way away, and you have to go through Sydney to get there. Most people don't make it past Sydney. I did – threw all my stuff in the back of a Greyhound and twenty four hours later I was in the thick of it, soaking up the angst, checking out the trams. I had a bedsit in East Melbourne.

Very few possessions. A typewriter. My old Japanese couch, which was actually a sort of black wooden park bench. A chest of drawers I found in the street, my mattress and this great Foster-Lindburgh bar fridge. I loved that fridge. It had rhythm. You'd hear it start and stop all night. About midnight it'd power up – *zhmmmmmmmm* – putting out those CFC's to chill my beers and cocktail onions. And at seven in the morning it'd switch off – the sudden absence

Andrew

One of the differences between Melbourne and Brisbane is the humble cockroach. It means the fry pan factor doesn't play as big a role in Melbourne as it does in some of the West End houses in Brisbane. In Brisbane if you leave a plate unwashed, you can go out four hours after everyone has gone to bed and the whole kitchen is moving around. In Melbourne you can leave your dinner scraps on the bench for two or three weeks and Old Mr Rat might have a go at it but that's about all. In winter it might even freeze, especially if you don't pay the power bills. Personal hygiene is not such an issue down south because people tend not to stink as much. I mean West End in summer? A house full of hard-core separatist lesbians? They can get bit whiffy.

of its warm familiar hum surprising me awake. It was a great little fridge and the best thing about it was the mondo cool badge on its door, half an eagle's wing like on the Harley Davidson motorcycles and the name Foster-Lindburgh spelt out in 1950's typography. I loved that fridge and I would have it with me now were it not for my insane neighbours who kidnapped it and took it on an adventure around town.

I was sharing my block of flats with Stacey, a *Melrose* kind of girl with no money whom I'd helped move into a unit directly upstairs from me. This crumbling unit block had been built for the American officers McArthur brought through in the Forties. It was worse than a gathering of former Soviet republics, torn asunder by untenable liaisons and messianic faction leaders. The macrodramatics were recreated in the daily theatre of life with Stacey, who feasted entirely on the exploits of others. She was jacked into a live feed from the Who Weekly Deathstar, so fully briefed on the lives of the world's fabulous young things that she could talk about them with the familiarity of a best friend from kindergarten. So it would be updates on Madonna, the lowdown on Gaultier, and a round-the-clock six channel datastream burst from the world-wide resources of the Sinead O'Connor bureau. Sinead O'Connor this, Sinead O'Connor that and Sinead O'Connor is very interesting because she shaves her head and has a lot to say. We were completely incompatible. I slept with her twice by mistake.

I tried to set Stacey up with Brendan, my friend the movie guy, in the vain hope that she might spend more time at his unit down the corridor. She resisted momentarily – said, 'Oh no no no … mmmh okay ' – then zeroed in on him at an art gallery launch. She said, 'You're cute, you make movies, take me home.' Brendan said 'Uhm uhm uhm … okay' and they wandered off together. Good deal. But when I got home I found they hadn't gone to his place, they were upstairs, thumping around on Stacey's bedroom floor like a pair of screeching baboons. Lots of moaning. Lots of 'Ohhhh Gods!' It went on and on. At that stage, I was just begining to scrape a living writing stories for trucking mags. I had a deadline that night but the bedroom gymnastics were giving me a serious case of mental block. Eventually, the moaning stopped upstairs and I heard the pitter-patter of little feet running down the hall, then a knock at my door. Stacey was standing there all breathless in black socks. Cheeks flushed. Hair a mess. She asked if the noise from upstairs was bothering me. 'Was it too loud?' You know, now that we had broken up and all? It wasn't disturbing my work or anything, was it? 'No,' I said. 'Great!' she smiled and pitter-pattered back up the hall. And they resumed. Louder and noisier than before. She did this every time I had a deadline. I'd be in my room pulling an all-nighter, the walls would be shaking and pounding, the baboons bellowing. Then silence. Pitter-patter pitter-patter down the hallway. Knock knock knock! 'Did you hear that?' Yes. 'We weren't disturbing you were we?' No. 'We were just having fun you know.' Yes I know. Please go away now. Pitter-patter pitter-patter and off they'd go again. I had to get out. The whole block of flats was charged with sexual tension – even the neighbours had a wild look in their eyes.

I packed everything into the back of a friend's car, everything but my beautiful black fridge, which wouldn't fit. That went under the stairwell of the adjacent block of flats where some other friends lived. Another *Melrose* situation. I got my gear to the new house in Fitzroy, crashed there that night and came back for the fridge the following morning. It was gone. Stolen. I was devastated, sitting on the steps with a black heart when Fletcher, this very rural down-to-earth character from the block next door, grabbed me and told me he'd been woken up at four in the morning by all this banging outside. Said he looked out the window and saw the girl upstairs and her bald-headed boyfriend making off with my fridge. They'd loaded it into the back seat of her station wagon and driven away with it. I charged up to her flat and knocked politely on her door. The girl answered.

'That old Holden wagon outside yours?' I asked cheerfully.

'Yes,' she answered just as brightly.

Bradley

The filthiest kitchen I ever saw was in my very
first flat. I shared with my mate Kevin. We were
the first of our crew to move out which meant that
everyone came to our place to hide and eat. We
made a big bowl of chilli the first night but
didn't eat it all. It just stayed on the stove
and grew a big thick green blue carpet of mould.
Because nobody wanted to clean it up we put it in
the cupboard with a lid on to see what would happen. Over the weeks it got furrier and thicker and
then even the mould started to die and go black.
Then when we peeled it back, the chilli underneath
still looked like chilli. It had not decayed at
all.
The dishes piled up like they do. There were times
we'd open the door, throw most of the them into
the yard and turn the hose on them. Spray everything down with a mixture of bleach and soapy
stuff, mop the walls. But it was just an inherently
unclean place.
The cockroaches lived behind the hot water system
in the kitchen. You'd switch the light out, get
the Glen 20 and wait. When you could hear them
you'd flick on the light, hold a cigarette lighter
up to the spray can and flame the roaches off the
wall. It was a lot easier than actually spraying,
which didn't really work anyway. >

'Can I have my fridge back then?' I asked, my voice shaking with anger.

Her face dropped. 'Oh no, I knew we'd get into trouble. I'll phone Ron up and get him to bring it back around.' I followed her in, we got Baldy on the phone and I asked for my fridge back. He shuffled and fumbled but there was no way out. I was going to get my fridge back – I was prepared to take his girlfriend *in lieu* if the thing wasn't at my new flat within a day. So I arranged to meet him at his place in the middle of the city, in this old warehouse, three storeys up, and helped him lug my fridge down all these flights of stairs and into his van. Pretty big of me I thought. But when I set it up in my new kitchen, I noticed that the Foster-Lindburgh badge was missing. I said to

> The wall didn't quite reach the floor between our kitchen and the place next door. There was about half a centimetre gap. Unfortunately we both put our bins there. The accumulation of garbage meant that if they didn't have maggots we did and because of the gap the little bastards would crawl through from one kitchen to the other. You could never keep control of them. We believed in hot water for maggot strikes. It poaches them, works faster than insecticide and petrol is bit rough inside the house. Bleach turns them into paste which gets into the cracks.
> It never resolved itself. We moved out.

Baldy, 'Where's the badge?' He shrugged, told me he had seen no badge. I looked at him very carefully. Thought, you are, after all, a fridge thief. But what am I going to do?

I reluctantly let it go, junked the fridge, continued my life without it. A couple of weeks later, I heard that Stacey had given Brendan the flick. (She'd said something like, 'You know what I like about you Brendan? You're a filmmaker. Filmmakers are cool.' And Brendan had sheepishly said something like, 'Actually, I'm not really a filmmaker, Stacey, I'm just a cameraman.' Stacey checked, found that cameramen were down pretty low on the credibility scale and Brendan had his marching orders the following day.)

Two years later, I'm back in Brisbane, but a magazine has sent me to Melbourne for a day, to do some story about yachting. I'm walking down Elizabeth Street and my eyes are drawn to this thing that looks exactly like my Foster-Lindburgh fridge badge. Coming towards me. It's just a glimpse in the crowd, but I follow it and discover it's attached to the bald fridge-stealer from my past. He's wearing my fridge badge as a belt buckle. He's converted my fridge badge into a fashion accessory. I grab Baldy by the shoulder and point down to the offending item. 'Hello – That's my fucking fridge badge!' Baldy stops, blusters and looks like he's going to have a little seizure on the footpath. And then he runs off. I chase the fridge-stealing bastard and tackle him on the other side of the road. I'm in this red mist, overwhelmed by images of beating him to death right there on the pavement. I must have looked insane because he gave in, undid the belt holding up his trousers and offered my fridge badge back to me. I carried it out of the city in triumph.

The house in Fitzroy was okay for a while. An old terrace I shared with Brian the electrician, Greg the gay school teacher, Agro the complete fool and Serina, a hellwoman from my past. I'd met her at a party and fallen headlong into her green eyes. Not a lot of pupil in those eyes, but it didn't matter. Her room was knee deep in rubbish and lit by a naked red lightbulb hanging from the ceiling. Her mattress was a gangrenous, mildewed slab of foam rubber without any sheeting. Pillows without pillow cases. A thin, stained doona with no cover, on to which she'd pile her clothes when it got really cold because she was a pin-eyed loner who made her own rules.

Serina appeared on my doorstep one morning in Melbourne, out of the blue. I hadn't seen her for the best part of a year. She told me she'd quit her job, had nowhere to go. I picked her bags off the footpath and carried them into my room. From that moment on, the house became great. Greg and Brian hit it off with Serina. She calmed right down, stopped the big drug binges. The sun shined on Melbourne for four solid months – and then it all turned to shit. A guy we knew called Nigel turned up at our door at two in the morning, soaking wet, having walked

Cheney

I haven't been in share housing much. I've had girlfriends I stayed with so I was the unauthorised long-stay boyfriend. It's good because you can see how a share house operates while having that safety hatch of being able to walk away. The main thing about share houses is that you're talking about loud people, when other people are trying to sleep. You're talking pubic hair in the shower. People can get over that. You're talking skid marks. You're talking seat up, seat down dilemmas. All that stuff. But the cause of destruction in most share houses is the fry pan. The humble fry pan. Someone will have a big greasy fry-up and the pan will just be left and left and left. Nobody will wash it up. I've seen people wash up everything in a share house. They'll wash up, they'll wipe the walls down, vacuum, but they'll just pretend the fry pan is not there. They work their way around it. I saw someone burst into tears once when they had to confront the fry pan.

through the rain after two days on a bus from Darwin. Nigel looked a bit like Nigel Havers, the champagne-drinking hurdle jumper from *Chariots of Fire*, but he also had that slightly disenfranchised manner of the deeply disturbed. He'd walked in on his girlfriend fucking another man in his bed and he snapped – ran away to Darwin for six months. Now here he was, standing in our doorway, a man in need. A happy constellation of events came together. We threw Agro out and I offered Nigel the spare room on the spot. Really pushed the deal for him.

Three days later, I had to go to Brisbane for a friend's wedding. As I was walking out the front door, I bumped into Nigel bundling his stuff in, loading it into Agro's room, next to Serina's and mine. It was a good moment in house history, a cheery back slapping interlude, but when I returned to Melbourne, the ambience had changed. Thrash music was pounding from the lounge room. Brian and Greg were on the edge, weirded out. Crazy stuff was happening and they didn't want to know about it. They'd been marginalised in their own house. So I read Serina's diary. I am one of those guys who will read your diary if you leave it around, and anyway it was pointless trying to talk to her, you couldn't get through the smoke screen.

The first entry read, *Went out with Nigel. He put the hard word on me. But I said no because I didn't want to be unfaithful to John.*

Okay. Cool. Three days later.

Nigel put the hard word on me again. I'd better not write any more.

Uh oh.

I didn't understand. I'd done a mate a favour and a

mate had done me wrong in return. I guess I should have taken to Nigel with a baseball bat – nobody would have thought less of me for it – but no one said anything and the house grew more and more evil. Nigel and Serina got into this conspiracy of drug use. Jacked themselves into the fabulous anti-glamour of it all. Serina was sleeping in my bed, but she didn't want to be there. And sleeping in a bed with a girl who doesn't want to be there is the absolute manifestation of Hell as we know it. There is nothing more painful than being next to the babe you love and knowing that if you touch her, she'll flinch. It's a fucking knife through your ribs.

The house collapsed during a hopeless night out when they insisted I score some speed for them. They shot it up. Shared the needle. Asked if I wanted some. I staggered off in horror, disappeared into the night. When I got home Serina's stuff had been moved out of my room and into Nigel's. He had been in the house for a total of two weeks. Greg and Brian were completely traumatised. Greg moved out. Brian went into shock. A great house had been fucked. And I had to find somewhere else to live in Melbourne. Fast.

I rang a number out of *The Age* share house section, got this guy out of bed at seven o'clock on a Saturday morning. Ernie in Carlton. He had a room going upstairs in a five bedroom terrace, but was thinking of renting out the living room too. It had a fire place and some big windows overlooking a leafy street. It was $45 a week, half a block to all the shops, but the best part was I said, 'I'll take it,' and he groggily goes, 'Oh, oh, oh, okay.'

There were some minor problems. The toilet was provincially located outside the house and they didn't have a fridge. But we overcame. We advertised to fill the last room with a hidden agenda that if someone mentioned they had a fridge they were in. We had the best ad on the window at Readings in Carlton. We had no problems with eating habits, sexual preference, race or gender. We just wanted a reasonable human being with a big fridge. We weren't fussy. It was a major error.

Within twenty-four hours of David moving in, the house was filling with smoke, ash trays and butts. This was a very nonconfrontational house. It took about two weeks for somebody, me I think, to point out to this guy that it had been a non-smoking place before he arrived and while we could bear him smoking in his room, it would actually be a lot cooler if he poisoned himself outside. After that, he'd light up just outside the kitchen but leave the door open and all the smoke would come through anyway. We gradually gave in, passively decided to become a smoking household because it was happening anyway. Then his girlfriend moved in. The girlfriend with a laundry fetish. Had to do it at least twice a day, every day. Sometimes more. Three in the morning, she'd be washing clothes in this old twin tub that had a high screaming whine when you ran the spin dryer.

Everybody except this idiot and his girl friend disappeared for Christmas – we all left to get away from them. The obscure PhD guy from the room in the roof went as far as Canada. He agreed to change rooms in his absence, because David's girlfriend was pissed off with having to live downstairs or something. I came back from a few days away and was going to do the right thing, give his room a quick vacuum. But I discovered there were four guys called Dave living in there. Another one, not called Dave, had squeezed in with David and his girlfriend, the mad washerwoman. One even brought his own telephone with him. Plugged it in and had it going the whole time. I tried to be diplomatic. Casually took David aside and said 'Martin's a pretty laid back guy. But I really think he'd be a bit concerned that four guys called Dave are living in his room while he's in Canada.' This presented no problem to David. He just moved all seven people into his own room.

It took about two weeks. Everyone complained in their own little groups, but nobody would actually challenge him. Then the phone bill came in with a five hundred dollar excess for the month and I fronted the guy, said 'Look, we've sort of decided you're going to have to move out.' It was an abhorrent thing to say because we'd been so cool about the way we ran the house. This guy was stunned. His jaw dropped. He was like, 'How can you do this? You utter bastard! What's the problem? We can talk

Joey

How do you avoid people you don't want to see?
There's always plenty of them. I lived in a huge
terrace in Footscray where the bedrooms were let
separately, so you'd never know who your housemates were going to be. I was studying Russian and
this fitted the atmosphere. Very bleak. Very
Dostoyevski. There was a wizened, alcoholic old man
who'd start up about eleven every night. You'd
hear the ring-pulls coming off his cans of beer
and then he'd start growling 'fucking cunt,' working himself into these drunken rages. There was a
woman who liked to stand by the door waiting for
someone to talk to. She'd tell you stories about
being a prostitute, really horrific stuff. If you'd
had a hard day, you'd walk in and get these stories about the negro sailor who fucked her so hard
she had to get a hysterectomy. You'd be pretty
well traumatised by the time you got away from
her. I had to work out how to get into the house
upon the sly. If she heard a creak she'd race out
and get you. I had a month of tip-toeing around
the back, coming in through the neighbour's yard,
climbing the fence. It was petrifying. You'd stand
on a creaky board and she'd get you. I knew every
fucking floor board in the place.

about it.' I got really hardline. We couldn't talk about it because as soon as we did, the salami tactics would start. One person might move out and there would only be six in the room. A negotiating move you know. This is a house that had six people on the lease, plus his girl friend, plus four Daves and a spare from Perth. It was pushing our rather minor facilities.

Somebody tried to alleviate the situation by saying, 'The problem is just that you don't clean, you don't pay bills and you're smoking the house out.' He said, 'Well I could start smoking outside again.' I said, 'No we really can't talk about this. You're going to have to move.' It was getting very tense. He said, 'Well, I'm not going to stay here if everybody doesn't want me to be here.' Two of my housemates, Mandy and Luke were passive people. They'd hide in their rooms, pull the shutters down while this whole thing was going on. Ernie had simply run away to Darwin, and I'm sitting there thinking, 'God, would anybody else like to solve this situation?'

In the end, I simply decided to disconnect the electricity, the gas and the telephone in a bid to freeze this turd out of the house.

I'm a survivor. I've lived without gas and electricity before. I can get by without the phone. Trouble is, the five Daves, the washerwoman and the spare from Perth really dug themselves in for a winter campaign. The house was freezing, but their cigarette smoke and body heat kept

David's room at a bearable temperature. They never came out. They were like the peasants, burning their cottages on the Russian front, and I'm like Napoleon watching my troops go down in the snow. Ernie never came back from Darwin. Mandy and Luke fell in love – drawn together by adversity – and found themselves a little loveshack in Prahran. I remember sitting in the living room, in the freezing cold, alone. It was my first Melbourne winter. I really understood the Leunig cartoons – all the black smoke and despair – and I suddenly snapped. 'Okay you bastards!' I started screaming. 'You win! It's yours!' I had the flu by this point, and moved out in a state of delirium. Threw most of my stuff away. Borrowed a mate's phone and took the first place that would have me.

A loft in Fitzroy.

A great building, but it wasn't so much a home as a dormitory. I never got to know everyone in the house. It had seven bedrooms, so at any one time there were at least ten people there, most of them mad, with one or two unclaimed mystery figures drifting around. Strangest of all was Benny the Londoner. He was thickset with short hair and gappy teeth and he had a really high-pitched voice. It was another house full of dope smokers but Benny didn't seem to do any drugs. He was on some weird hormonal trip. He was evil. I figured that out on the second or third night, while a few of us were watching *Blade Runner* on video – there's this scene where Harrison Ford shoots an android girl in the back and she crashes through a bunch of plate glass windows in slow motion, wearing nothing but a see-through plastic raincoat. Great big holes in her back. Lots of blood. I looked across at Benny and he had the horn. Right there in his pants – and a really big grin frozen on his face. In his quiet, high-pitched voice, he said, 'I love to see a bitch go down.' Scared the hell out of me. A few nights later everyone was bagging some girl who used to live there. Benny got the same big grin. Said his fantasy was to give her a thousand paper cuts. 'All over her body.' It just came out of the blue. Creepy.

Brendan

There were four of us living in St Kilda. A student, a chef, a doley and Leo, whose parents owned restaurants. Leo drove the delivery van and had a lucrative sideline in black market food. Seeing as Scott was a chef he'd pinch mountains of stuff on Fridays for our regular Saturday night feasts. We'd have these incredible dinners even though we were broke. Atlantic salmon. Smoked venison. Bottles of Krug and Grange Hermitage. You'd wake up on Sunday morning there'd be a dozen people crashed out on the floor of this awful flophouse.

I decided to suss out his room while he was away for a day. It was neat. Minimalist. Clothes folded and tucked under the bed. Nothing on his shelves. Cupboards locked. A cheap cane table beside his bed. Resting on that, an old photograph of man in naval uniform, which I took to be of his Dad, and a pair of handcuffs.

I had the room next to this guy. The wall between us was a fibro sheet, nailed up at some stage in the past. I could hear him breathing sometimes. Cherie his horror girlfriend brought another girl home late one night. I saw Benny, Cherie and this other girl disappear into his room. I got into bed and lay awake for an hour waiting for the sex noises or even the sound of them leaving. But not a sound came from that room. It was absolutely quiet. Like, David Lynch *Blue Velvet* quiet.

We had a house dinner the following evening. Steve set it up. He had the lease on the house or owned it or something. The arrangements were nonspecific. Whatever. By sheer mismanagement, he'd let these weirdoes move in and run the place down. He finally insisted on this pot luck curry as a bonding experience, so we all sat round at the big dining room table: Steve; his lumpy live-in girl friend; the go-getting babe from Warrnambool; some roadie for The Mutant Shitbags; the two pot-smoking feral girls; Angie, the stringy-haired girl who really liked an awful cover band called Snailz Trailz and always wore their tee shirts; myself; and Benny.

It was a dismal failure. We had nothing to bond over. Frequent and cramped silences strangled any fellow feeling. Out of sheer nervousness, I had a few drinks and starting handing a bit of shit about. I had a bit of a lend of Benny and he went very quiet. After five or six drinks, I had to go to the toilet which was on the top floor. I walked up the first flight of stairs, the second, the third, the fourth, went into the bathroom and had a piss. While I'm standing there Benny slipped in behind me and shut the door. In his high-pitched voice this short Londoner said, 'I tell you Johnny if you ever do that again I'll kill you.' He meant it too. It was all in the eyes. Everything you needed to know right there. Had those flat, reptilian eyes. I stammered a heart-felt apology and moved out three days later.

a modern aesthetic

Voices of the Damned

Jack

<u>TRUST NOBODY.</u>

There are some flatmates who
never seem to have the money to pay
their bills. There are other flatmates
who will use your money to pay their
bills. And there are those very special
flatmates who will steal your money
and leave town, still not having
paid their bills.

JACK NOW WORKS FOR THE
AUSTRALIAN BUREAU OF CRIMINAL
INTELLIGENCE WHERE HIS HOBBY
IS TRACKING DOWN THIS
PREVIOUS FLATMATE.

There were three of us living in Bondi, myself, my girlfriend Ros and Lizzy, a friend of hers. We wanted to let the spare room to bring down the rent because we were saving for our wedding. After interviewing a couple of weirdoes we took this guy who said he was a chef. He was 21, a surfer type, didn't have much stuff, had just moved from Adelaide. He said he was trying to see the country by working his way around.

He was always late with the rent and we were constantly chasing him up. He said he got paid at a different time from the rest of us so we ended up not paying the rent in one slab. We'd pay ours and he was supposed to put his in later. We only discovered the problem when I went down to pay the rent personally. Usually we just put it in a bank account. He was about $1200 behind. He paid some of that off but slipped behind again, kept making excuses. 'I'll get the money. I'll get the money.' He was slow chipping in for bills. The electricity was virtually impossible to get out of him. Like pulling teeth. 'I'm running short right now but I got money coming next week,' and so on. The whole time he's buying stuff like a new surf board, a

new guitar, he's on the piss every night
of the week. Then I noticed that all the
gold coins were disappearing from the
phone box. And my girlfriend 'lost' the
gold coins from her purse a couple of
times.
He was working nights so he'd be going out
as we were coming home. We noticed one
night that he and one of his mates were
talking in his room about moving out
together. He didn't say anything to us and
he wasn't broadcasting this discussion
through the house. We just overheard him.
We were driving through Bondi shortly
afterwards and saw him and this mate
checking out the rental boards at a real
estate agency.
He finally told us he'd be moving in a
couple of weeks. We came home the next day
and he was gone. We checked the rent. He
owed $1100 there. He hadn't paid any gas
or electricity, they ran to about $300.
His share of the phone bill came to $700.
I rang a couple of the numbers from the
phone bill, thinking they might have an
address for him but they didn't know or
didn't let on. I found his mother and
explained that we wanted the money. She
said he was somewhere in Queensland but

she didn't know where. We traced him to
Noosa, and then to a caravan park outside
Cooktown but the trail went cold. He left
us a stained futon mattress and a couple
of old sandshoes.

the ACID in

your stomach

would burn a

HOLE in the

carpet

NO JUNKIES

Some truths are self evident. You're never going to measure up in the sack with a girl whose first name is Sweden. And the arrival of a junkie spells certain death, even for the most liberal household. A junkie it was went belly up on my favourite green bean bag. A junkie it was ran a huge credit scam out of my house. Unpaid bills? Missing teaspoons? Stolen CD's? I think we all know who's responsible.

I did the lounge room floor circuit after Melbourne. Eventually wound up back in Brisbane, in the front room of a huge place, high up on stumps in Birdwood Tce, Auchenflower. This was the house where we pulled a dozen cones and planted a fresh vegie patch in the backyard, wearing goldfish-bowl space helmets. (We awoke the following morning, and discovered we had planted three perfectly symmetrical rows of lettuce and spinach.) This was the house of the Kinky Sex house-warming party – dozens of people scarfing up $50 ecstacy tabs like Smarties and fanging around in G-strings and dog collars, while two gay boys from the country in leather jocks and Spartacus sandals held a whip-cracking competition out on the road. This was the house of the winter solstice blue moon party, when we set fire to the Hills Hoist and performed a slow-motion Satanic Mass in the backyard. (My friend Wayne, who dabbled in the black arts as an adjunct to his veterinary practice, cast a spell on the Hoist, which we'd wrapped in metho and detergent-soaked rags. When we set it alight and spun it around, the whole thing went up like a burning blue firewheel, dripping and spitting little meteors of flame.) This was the house where you had to sit directly in front of the teev, because we'd collected dozens of cardboard tubes from the inside of toilet rolls and stuck them onto the screen to break the picture down into a fantastic swirling kaleidoscope of tiny TV circles. (It makes a lot of sense when you're ripped.) And this was the house where we consumed inhuman amounts of hashish and mescal, went on the mother of all adventures and ended up getting busted by the cops for making off with the pot plants outside Bjelke-Petersen House. (We were charged with stealing two maidenhair ferns to the value of not more than fifteen dollars.) This was not a house which was down on drugs. But we did have one rule.

Margi

We had a flatmate who loved to go clubbing on Oxford Street. One night he was walking home, snorting amyl, and he tripped. The amyl went right up the back of his nose, so when he got home he was walking very oddly. He crashed to the kitchen floor. I got up to find him on the tiles, thought he was having a bad acid trip and I'd have to see him through. I'm patting his hand, saying you'll be all right, you'll be fine. He looked me in the eyes, said 'Tell my mother I'm sorry' and turned blue. We had a first-year nursing student living there so I started screaming for her and rang the ambulance. We had no idea what he was on. The ambulance guys are going 'Is he smacked out' and we're saying 'No no he doesn't use smack'. So they took him away and pumped his stomach. He swore later that two orderlies at the hospital had a play with his thing while he was non compos. We picked him up about six in the morning. Brought him home. We're all sitting in the kitchen, feeling awful and he said 'Fuck I had great time last night'. And he went out clubbing the next night.

No junkies.

I moved into this house during a hail storm. Vaguely knew Danny, one of the guys there. Friend of a friend sort of thing. Wound up on my first night sitting on the verandah with Danny and his housemates Margot and Wayne, drinking hot sweet tea and passing a joint around, nobody talking, as we watched the storm build up way out over the western ranges, raising a dark, monstrous anvil in the sky, filling the air with crackling ozone and static and a weird green light that rendered things flatter and harder than they really were. As it closed down on us, we could see the lowest tiers were boiling and swirling and carrying the whole storm system along on a fast running stream of mottled sick yellow sky. I reached for the Tim Tams as the first hail stones began bouncing off our corrugated iron roof. Trees bent. The wind briefly whipped up a dusty twister of leaves and old chip packets and a sheet of newspaper, sent them whirling across our front path just before the sky cracked open and fell in on our house.

'Hope the bitch is out in it,' said Margot.

The bitch was Wayne's ex-girlfriend. She had moved into his room, refusing to pay any rent or bills. It wasn't like she was still going out with him or anything. She'd bring home other guys and fuck them in his bed. She'd be in there thrashing around under the sheets, and poor old Wayne would be jackknifed on the two seater lounge outside, listening to the whole thing.

Her name was Kristin.

When she went off to work, Kristin was Anya. She ran a schizoidal relay between the two identities. It was Anya who dressed up and went off to the whorehouse, Kristin who came home and jacked herself up a few spoons of smack. She had a very English demeanour, very Sloane Square, Wimbledon, strawberries and cream, but it was twisted. She fucked strange men for money. She liked to brag about making $1600 on a Friday night. She was like – 'I make all of this money' and Wayne and Danny and Margot were like, 'Well why don't you buy some groceries?' She was bludging off an Austudy house full of dishwashers and mop jockeys. They found out later she'd just been tossed out of a flat in Toowong, because some of her drug buddies had turned the place over.

Like I said, the house didn't have many rules. Only one really. No junkies. No intravenous drugs in the house. That lasted about two days. Then Kristin went on a five week smack binge. She was on a methadone program, which meant she was doubly out of it, doubly awful, all the time. She'd come up for air every couple of days – 'Oh I've given up now' – never cooked, never cleaned, had these oily baths. Left the tub full of cold, grey, greasy water. Came home all hours, cranked the stereo up when everyone was trying to sleep. Full bore. Courtney Love and Hole.

She'd bring her smack friends around to shoot her up. Said it was more fun than doing it yourself. So this

Dave

Pat, his mate Raj and a couple of guys from McDonald's where he worked liked to come home and get into heaps of buckets. After three or four quick buckets each they'd then knock down about fifty bulbs of nitrous. There were always hundreds of nitrous bulbs scattered around our house. The guys'd be totally fucked. Muted. Once, Pat was standing by the French windows when he took in this bulb and started staggering backwards. He crashed through the doors, still going backwards, couldn't get his balance and fell off the verandah. His legs whipped through air and the last thing we saw of him were the soles of his shoes as he went down like Wile E. Coyote. He hit the driveway and lay there doing spasms but because he was totally wasted he was also totally relaxed so he survived.

circus came to the living room. They'd fix themselves up while Danny, Margot and Wayne are trying to have dinner. Typical junkies. Laying the implements out on the coffee table. Asking if you could hold their arms for them. You'd roll your eyes in weary contempt. But Kristin would breathe, 'When I'm on heroin I know all the answers.' She sounded like an ad campaign.

Heroin. All the Answers!

And the drama of hanging out for it. Obsessing about it for hours, getting worked up, stressed out, ringing up, hanging out, waiting for it waiting for it waiting for it waitingforitwaitingforit … Aaaah! It's here! 'I know all the answers.' And then coming down and being even more unbearable. Then she started fucking a dealer, and the next thing they know, there's a pipeline of pure shit pouring straight into their living room.

It wasn't just her. It was her whole family. They were always coming around. Her brother, the young yuppie try-hard. Brown leather jacket, blue chambray shirt. Fancied himself a bit of an operator.

'I can get five thousand eccies at two bucks a pop.'

Her father was a cop, deep into reality denial about his little girl. He was on duty when Kristin turned up in Casualty with a gutful of pills. He kept the CPR team working on her. Fuck it, they said, what's the point? But Kristin's dad insisted they bring his daughter back from the dead.

The house finally gave her a week's notice. At the end of that week there's an empty suitcase on the lounge room floor, but no movement on the Departures Board. So they started throwing her stuff in. Figured she'd come home from the brothel and get the message. But no. She got home, turned the stereo up, made herself a double cheese omelette. Margot lost it in her room across the hallway, reefed back the bed sheets, stomped into the living room and went her like a pit bull terrier. Sharp teeth. Bad scene.

Kristin tried to get a word in, you know, tell her side of the story but Margot was off, screeching like a six foot tall vampire bat in fluffy slippers, reaching into the bottomless pit of Kristin's crimes and outrages. Her selfishness. Her laziness. Her three hours showers. Her totally tragic, regularly scheduled, pantomime suicide vanity trips. Her telling Wayne, the dish-washing ex-boyfriend whose bed she had annexed, that his life was insignificant compared with hers and that looking at him made her want to throw up. Wayne, Margot screamed, was a hundred times the person she'd ever be, she was, 'a … a … a … slut … junkie … bushpig!' Before Kristin could do or say anything in reply, Margot picked up her suitcase, tore down the hallway and launched it off the front steps. The house was set high. The suitcase arced through the air for a good ten seconds before it hit the ground, long enough for Kristin to disappear through the back door and out into the night. When Margot stormed back into the house, she was gone. I moved in the following day.

The hailstorm passed. Steam rose from the bitumen. Soil and plants and even the boards of the house exuded a rich smell of rot and genesis, as juicy and tactile as the syrup seeping from the fissures in the fat, over-ripe mangoes which lay at the foot of the tree in the farthest reaches of the backyard. One of those curiously suspended moments had overtaken the verandah. So we talked a bit – me, a vague acquaintance, and two complete strangers. Beyond a certain level of personal hygiene and financial probity, one of the most sought-after qualities in a potential flatmate is the ability to hold up their end of a conversation. Nobody likes to have a silent, brooding presence on the brown

Scot

My friend Reg moved in with a scrupulously tidy guy, a real nice guy too. Reg was a real smoker, a stick-a-day man. The cops came around during Operation Noah. Say they've received information and they want to search the place. They go to Reg's room, it's like a black hole. They can't even get in because of this cupboard pushed up against the door. Reg had to climb over it to get in and out, and beyond that it's just chaos. The cops say, 'You could have a plantation in there mate and we'd never find it.' So they go to Steven's bedroom, which is scrupulously tidy of course, and they tear it apart. And at the back of his underwear draw they found fifty seeds. They weren't even his. They were left-overs from some previous tenant. That's how he got his conviction. And Reg of course did have half an ounce stashed away at the time, but they were never going to find it in that room.

couch when visitors call or the bong is passed round. Still, you'd be amazed at the number of angry loners you find bunking down in share accommodation. Would those Gun Lobby types be so gung-ho if they'd spent some time backed up against a bedroom wall, watching a two dollar latch buckling under the shoulder charges of a savagely drunk taxi driver in camouflage pants and a Death Before Dishonour tee shirt? I don't think so.

Danny's nickname was Decoy. He was a nice guy, one of the best, but terrible things kept happening to him. He used to live in this really big house with only one sane person in it — himself. All the others were in various degraded phases of alcoholism and drug addiction. They ranged in severity from being into their second week on the grog and going at it straight because it was still so much fun, through to the stage where you didn't want to know where their rent money came from. When you took it off them you handled it with gloves, put it into a plastic evidence bag. His room was a little island in this sea of madness. It was a nice room. Looked out over the front street in Highgate Hill. Great views. The house itself had faulty wiring, broken windows and a toilet that backed up all the time. The run-off seeped through the floor and flowed through the backyard. His junkie flatmates had stolen a little bridge from a park, thrown it over this flow, and put a sign up: Cholera Creek.

Cholera Creek was an infamous house around those

parts. On top of being addicted to various drugs, the residents were very unwisely involved in lots of radical political groups. Expo '88 was bearing down upon Brisbane at that time. There was a lot of opposition to it around that part of town. Before Danny's house was raided, there had been stories about other houses in the neighbourhood being torched. The inference was that the cops were involved. The links were never made clear, it was just one of those Brisbane things.

Anyway Danny's sitting in his room one day. He looks out the window and there are six or seven cops on the front stairs. He runs out to warn everyone in the house, but it's too late. Another half dozen cops have gone around the back and are swarming in through the kitchen. They were mostly uniformed, but they had a couple of suits with them. Miraculously, nobody had any drugs in the house. The cops claimed they were looking for guns. Said the neighbours had reported hearing gunfire in the area. They gave a big speech about the guns and said, 'Do you have any guns on the premises?' Then they took away some address books, some posters and stuff. They loved the posters. These militant things from the UK with aggressive slogans on them about killing cops and smashing the State. A few days later, Danny's walking around town when this car pulls up. Two suits jump out, grab him and wrestle him into the car. He recognises one of these plain clothes guys as this infamous character who'd been under suspicion for

Cameron

I resigned from a job in Toowoomba, broke up with a girl, piled everything I owned into a car and drove down to Sydney. I arrived with $110 on me. I rang a name I knew and asked for a job. He got me on as a shift manager with this chain restaurant in Pitt Street. I lived in my car for the first few weeks, parked it up near Mrs Macquarie's Chair. The first person I met at this food joint was an employee who dragged me over to a table, sat me down and got me something to eat. His name was Gerald. I soon realised this guy had just been sacked, but I sat there and finished my sandwich.

About two weeks went by with me living in this car before Gerald came by and >

the murder of an Aboriginal girl. They called him the lady killer. He grabs Danny's wrist and holds it up for his mate to see. He says to his mate, 'Look at this Terry, he's got the tremors. I reckon he's on something. What do you think?.' And Terry replies, 'I reckon we'd better search his house, mate. Looks like there could be drugs there.'

Danny tells them he's not going anywhere unless he's formally arrested and charged, you know, the usual spiel. But the cops seem to know everything about him. They're saying, 'That's a pity Francis, because it'd be a bit rough wouldn't it? A chap like you spending the weekend in the watchhouse. With your medical condition?

> asked if I wanted to move out. He'd got a job as
a kitchen-hand in some swish restaurant. I was
pretty keen to get out of the car so we took a
flat in Cronulla.

I was working two jobs at this stage, so when
Gerald asked what I wanted for dinner in the morning I said groggily, 'Well I'm thinking Veal Cordon
Bleu.' He said, 'Well fuck, that sounds all right
to me'. I came back after work and our fridge was
full. I mean it was just full of wine, fruit,
sweets, and meat. This stuff was obviously hot,
pinched from his workplace, and I tried to dis-
courage him. But the fridge just got fuller and
fuller. We were starting to throw out the smoked
salmon and French pate. He was compulsive. There
was nothing I could do so I ate the evidence.
The crunch came when I realised that he was seriously klepto. We went into a Shell servo to get
some change and when we pulled out I couldn't see
with the rear vision mirror. In the time I'd taken
to change my money he'd shovelled anything within
arm's length onto the back seat. Soccer balls.
Crates of Coke. Rolls of paper. And these pine
trees. Three of them. I asked him what the fuck he
thought he was doing and he said 'Don't worry I
got you some oil for your car'. I fled before the
cops turned up.

Anything could happen in there.' And Danny's eyes have gone wide, because the cops are calling him Francis – only his parents know his christian name, everyone else calls him Danny – and they're talking about his allergy to an epilepsy drug which could kill him if administered by mistake. 'Friday afternoon?' the lady killer is saying. 'Court doesn't come up until Monday. You'd have a whole weekend in the watchhouse.' He's saying this in a genuinely concerned voice. 'It's a long time until Monday. Anything could happen. And let's face it Francis. It probably will. Won't it?'

So Danny agrees to take them to the house. Before he gets out of the car, he suggests that he'd better go first, because someone in the house had a Doberman and the dog was quite vicious. If it saw strangers it might attack them. 'No worries,' says the lady killer and pulls a firearm out of a holster. But not dramatically, you understand. Not like on TV or anything. He just pulls it out the same way we'd get a cheese stick from the fridge, and leads Danny around the side of the house. It was one of those houses where the front door had been boarded up and the verandah converted into a long skinny sleepout. You can't lock the back door, so they go into the house and start looking around. One of them radios for back-up, asks for the dog squad as well. Danny's really sweating at this stage, and turns on Four Triple Zed, the local left-field public radio station, to mask his panic. And he can hear one of his flatmates on the air. She's hosting Prisoners Hour. Very ironic. The girl's on the radio, and then in this typical bumbling public radio way, she says she's left one of her records at home, 'I'll just call to see if anyone can bring it around to the studio.' Danny freezes. And the phone rings. The cops are preoccupied, they don't attend to the radio. They just nod to Danny to answer the phone. He snatches it up and blurts into it that the police are raiding the house. 'Broadcast it!' he cries 'Ring my solicitor. Get help fast.' The cops come over in this quiet fury, just as Danny's flatmate comes back on the radio in a gust of excitement – 'Hey everybody! My house is being raided! We'll bring it to you live!'

When the phone rings again it's Danny's solicitor. Danny is feeling a little cockier now and he answers, 'West End Police Station?'

'Ah don't mate. Don't make a joke of it. You're in deep shit,' says the brief. She asks to talk to a cop. Danny hands the phone over. The killer's talking and nodding and going 'Yes, yes, no, no, yes. That's correct.' Then he starts arguing, saying, 'We have every right to be here.' And then there's the sound of feet thundering up the back stairs – Danny thinks it's the dog squad, but it's six spaced-out people with tape recorders who've run half way across the suburb. They say they're from Triple Zed and hit the record buttons of their machines. There are microphones everywhere. Terry, the rookie, doesn't know what to do, so he says, 'I'm arresting you all.' A guy with a tape recorder says, 'He's arresting us all,' and the lady killer gets off the phone, gets on his radio and says, 'Negate that request for dog squad and back up.' There are witnesses and live microphones everywhere so the cops leave. But as they walk out the door, the lady killer taps Danny on the chest and whispers into his face – 'You made a big mistake Francis.'

Danny sees out the rest of the day at that house in a fairly blank state – another twenty people with tape recorders turn up, and when they see there are no police around, they decide to break out the drugs and have a party. The party goes on all night – but at the crack of dawn,

Darryl

```
I moved into a house which had a bed that killed
people. The other people living there said some
girl had inherited it after her grandmother died
in her sleep. She was strangled to death in it
about six months later. After the guy that
replaced her overdosed in the bed, they wanted to
throw it away, but one of the other guys twisted
his ankle trying to manoeuvre it down the stairs.
That bed wasn't going anywhere. It had tasted
human flesh.
```

Danny throws all his gear into the back of his clapped-out Combi, and drives down to the Gold Coast, where he hides out for a couple of months.

Margot wound up at the house on account of Lucinda the loon. She'd been living over in St Lucia in a place with a spare room, which the household had decided to advertise through Triple Zed's accommodation notices. Used all the codewords. 'Green leafy suburb', 'Open minded'. But they had a brutally straight-forward 'No Junkie' embargo on the place. Well, Lucinda drops in for an interview and seems okay. She's no junkie. She's been living with her mother for three months. They found out later that she'd actually been locked up in a mental hospital for smack addiction and schizophrenia.

Being a complete loon and addicted to both theatrics and heroin, Lucinda would play out these schizodramas on a day-to-day basis. One morning, Margot wakes up to this unholy screaming in the bathroom. She runs in to find Lucinda in tears, shaking uncontrollably because someone had spat in the bath. Margot tells her it's okay, reassures her, strokes her hair, turns on the taps and washes it away. That afternoon the phone rings, a call for Lucinda. Margot goes into her room – 'Lucy. Phone for you' – but Lucinda is on the floor, groaning about 'too many pills'. Her little white arm snakes out from under her doona and knocks over a half empty bottle of Melarol. Margot hits panic mode, calls a friend in drug counselling and asks what these Melarol tablets are supposed to do. The drug counselling guy says they won't kill her but the house would have to look after her for about twenty-fours hours. So the whole house goes on Lucinda Watch.

Now, Lucinda was a champagne lesbian – it was more fashion statement than sexual thing – but she had a lovely girlfriend who would occasionally disappear up north. When this happened, Lucinda would go into depression overdrive and start bringing home strangers to share her bed. Man, woman or beast, she didn't care. Then one day Margot's flatmate Andrew is knocking on her door, and says Lucinda has been in the bathroom for a very long time. He's starting to worry. So they check it out. There's steam coming out under the door, they know she's in there, but it's really quiet. She's not responding when they call. Doesn't even splash. In the end, Andrew kicks the door off its hinges and they burst in.

Lucinda is lying in the bath. The bath is full of blood. The first thought that rockets through Margot's mind is that she's slashed her wrists. But she hasn't. Andrew pulls her arms out of the water and they're uncut. They drain the bath and discover the truth. Lucinda had gotten herself pregnant to some Maori bouncer and decided to give herself a home abortion. She'd taken five or six packets of the pill all at once, and had a miscarriage in the bath. So Andrew drags Lucinda out of the bathroom and into an ambulance and leaves Margot to clean up the mess. There's some residue clogging up the plughole, so Margot puts her hand in a plastic garbage bag and fishes around in the bloody water. Her fingers close around a handful of pulpy matter and she pulls it out and looks at it. It's been ripped to pieces by the end of a coathanger. And that's it for Margot and the house – every time she tries to take a bath, the torn thing is in there with her. She lasted three weeks without washing, and then she hit the road.

Recreational Drug Use Area.

Voices of the Damned

Mark

<u>HEROIN. ALL THE ANSWERS!</u>

Apart from Scientologists and
born-again Christians, junkies are
probably the worst people in the
world to live with. Even other
junkies will tell you that.

MARK IS STILL ALIVE.
HE NOW EDITS A
MAJOR FASHION MAGAZINE.

I'm the dickhead in this story. Despite maintaining a terrible drug habit I liked a tidy house. It was probably my method of pretending everything was all right when I was fucked on the drugs. But it would cause tension when I was living with other junkies who didn't give a shit. I went mad over this kitchen in Kings Cross. Domestic things were just instinctive to me. Cooking and cleaning and so on. But nobody else got into it because they were all young and drug-fucked. I went completely insane. It was a butter and milk impasse which got to me. It drove me insane that I could never have soft butter. I liked to keep the butter out of the fridge and the milk in the fridge. I finally put this huge notice in the kitchen: PUT THE FUCKING MILK BACK IN THE FRIDGE. LEAVE THE FUCKING BUTTER OUT OF THE FRIDGE. Very, very uncool. I suffered a lot of harassment over that. I became the laughing-stock of the house.

Years later when my life and drug habits had degenerated in tandem I was living in Roslyn Gardens, where Paul Keating has a place now. This was with a bunch of girls. I mostly tended to live with girls. It was one of those things. The stereotype of men being totally unhouse-trained is so often

accurate. All-male households are usually
frat house beer dens, which is pretty unen-
durable for a guy who puts up signs about
the milk and butter. As a young bloke I
looked at that slob archetype lifestyle,
which was supposedly so rebellious, and I
just wanted to tidy up the kitchen.
There were two of us maintaining covert
habits in this house. One of the girls,
let's call her Alice, started to screw the
dealer. I then figured she had lots of
smack and I had an excuse to steal it. I'd
hang around when she went out. Wait a
while. And as people tend to hide these
things in pretty obvious and consistent
places I'd then find her smack and take it.
It was like a welfare supplement for my own
habit. I lived for a long time like that.
I had to skip on that place because a couple of fraud jobs caught up with me. If
you're going to get into the smack and you
don't want to get into mugging or break-
and-enter it virtually ensures that you
will become involved in credit fraud. And
fraud inevitably involves skipping on share
house arrangements. I had recently skipped
on a place and they traced me because I
took everything but a bag of garbage which
contained a letter with a return address
for my brother. The cops showed up and took

me away. They had a huge file on me but
they couldn't make it add up exactly so
they let me go.
I drifted for a while. Just took couches
and temporary beds with friends. Then I
moved into a friend's house in Nimrod St.
Kings Cross with a couple of noted thespian
types. It was another terrible drug saga.
These were bacchanalian thespians. They
loved to smoke joints, eat cheese and drink
red wine. I was into heroin, leather pants
and rock and roll. I guess they thought
this was a touch of glamour and danger
under their roof. Then the reality hit
them.
They were all sitting around one night
smoking and throwing back the plonk and the
King Island brie. I came home with Michael
and Sonya, some guys from my band. We'd had
a really good gig so Michael and I had gone
out and scored. Sonya was quite mild-man-
nered, didn't do smack at all. But Michael
and I disappeared into my room, took this
dope and were completely flattened by it.
Michael just dropped, all but dead on the
floor. I could see he had overdosed and
wasn't breathing but I was so out of it I
honestly didn't give a shit. I shambled
into the living room to find Sonya, who was
like the bridge between us and the thespi-

ans, and mumbled, 'Eh Sonya.. come 'ere." I
pointed to Michael and turned my back on
him, walked out into the living room, into
this collection of polite people and
flopped in a chair, a drooling, drop-lidded
vision of horror. I had a cigarette burning
down to my fingers and picked up the near-
est bottle of whatever was going. Sonya
bolted out ... 'Fuck fuck fuck!!! Michael's
dead!'
These people had never seen anything like
it. Michael had to be brought to. I think
we succeeded without the help of the ambulance. After he comes to we partied for
ages. The next morning my thespian friend
put his head round the door and politely
says 'Uhm Mark, I think uhm ...' I put my
hand up, 'Don't worry mate. I've got a new
place. I'll be gone by lunch time.' He was
very relieved.
That's how I ended up with these two gay
guys. The problem was that I was a bit
boofy, you know. I'm sort of blokey and I
like to spend the weekends in front of the
telly watching the footy and I think it got
to the guys. That was an aspect of my blok-
iness that just wasn't going to work in a
gay house. So I was asked to leave under
the pretext that I spent too much time

there. I said, 'But while I'm spending time
here I'm doing the cooking and the cleaning
up.' Didn't matter.

I ended up on a friend's couch after that.
I was there for a while but he was a bed
smoker. He set his futon on fire one night.
I was pinned so I slept through most of
the emergency but when he woke me up the
place was pretty much wrecked by futon
smoke and water damage. My friend was pack-
ing shit so we borrowed a ute, this is at
three in the morning, threw everything in
the back and fled. I was getting pretty
tired of this by now. I was a man on the
run. So I went the whole hog. Sold my gui-
tars and bought a ticket to London.

NORTHERN GOTHIC

The house sat on the edge of a monstrous freeway development, just outside the city. An overpass had been rammed through the front yard, so the owner didn't really care what happened to the place. He just wanted whatever rent he could get, which wasn't that much because the house was full of Goths. Being out of contact with reality, Goths tend to neglect the mundane things in life like paying the rent, and when the estate agents got serious and sent the strong arm boys around, the little vampire colony was $4200 in arrears.

I'm not sure how many people lived there. There

were three regulars and lots of drop-ins. Kevin the carpenter – plying his trade in a completely dark room lit by candles – had a great cordless drill. When I asked if it was powerful enough, he said 'Fuck yes!' turned around and started drilling holes in the wall. The teev was turned on all the time but only half tuned so that the picture could distort in time to the beat of Front 242 and Revolting Cocks which screamed out of the stereo pretty much incessantly. I met an apprentice printer from the front room who was totally hung up on Laibach, this Yugoslavian band. They were a blood and soil act. Played a lot of new Nazi anthem stuff, wore big deer antlers and crap on stage. They were not actually fascist themselves, you understand, it's just an art thing, called New Slovenian Art. Of course you can't say New Slovenian Art in English. You have to say it in the original language because that's all part of the art. There was a bald guy who lived out the back. Totally serious about his image, shaved his head, wore black eyeliner everywhere. He rarely ever paid for anything, denounced property as unimportant. Very snobbish and elitist. Hardly saw him speak a word to anyone. And there was another guy called Luke who was said to be into creating music, but the only thing that he'd really done was drill off-centre holes in his collection of old 45s. He'd whack them on the record player and sit there all night, thrilled with the discovery that the music speeds up and slows down and speeds up and slows down and speeds up and slows down. Infinitely. Actually the whole household was pretty excited about that.

But the strong arm boys came down heavy and they all skipped on me one night – took off like a swarm of bats flying out from Indooroopilly Island. My name wasn't on the lease and I more or less took the frighteners in my stride – strong arm men don't bother me anymore, you just look blank and dead and disinterested at them long enough, and they eventually realise that beating you up would be very, very boring – so I wound up with the house to myself. Good deal. I set up camp. Found a table to put my typewriter on. Bought some groceries. Thought about life for a while. Then the extended family that is Brisbane sent some people along to keep me company, and for my sins, I took them in.

Dirk was a funny little dude. I told you about him

Sam

Goths have a great hide-and-seek party game. You put on really loud music, so loud you can barely hear yourself think. Everyone has two or three bongs. You extinguish all candles. The house is blacked out, like jet black, then one person hides. Everyone goes looking for the hider. But when they find the hider they don't say anything. They quickly crawl into the hiding place with them. This goes on until one person is left, stoned as hell, careening around the dark, empty house.

earlier. Remember? Thought cleaning the bathroom was a heterofascist plot? Well Dirk had this strange hair. Sort of a mutant afro. He told me once that he really wanted hair like the guy from *Eraserhead* but that rather than growing up in a curly high rise, it grew out. A tragedy. He came with two women – Em, a banker and still one of my best friends, and Crazy Nina, a complete disaster, one of the most deranged people I have ever lived with in my whole life.

We had a great housewarming party. One of those parties that came in human waves – bingeing crims, yuppie yobboes, professional crashers, hopeful punters, crazy ferals, angry punks, hairy freaks, girly swots, naive schoolies, cynical journos, screaming fags and sweaty dykes, bent cops, backdoor specialists, conquering heroes and hopeless jokes, great pretenders, pale imitators, smooth operators, and even some of the vampire bats who did a runner on this house in the first place. People got drunk and scaled the hall. Feet on one side, arses on the other. There were a dozen of us, leg to leg up there, weeping drunk, bottles in our laps, girls over our knees. We didn't come down for some time and the walls were permanently bowed afterwards. People went tripping, naked in the bath, just lying there, with a little water dripping on their heads. A couple of chemists made up a half kilo block of potassium nitrate and sugar smoke mix. A chunk the size of your thumb will fill an ordinary room. There were nitrous tanks and hydrogen balloons. Tied them off, attached a fuse, lit them up and let them go. Boom! The front stairs collapsed, but some builders made temporary stairs out of stolen milk crates. Meanwhile there's this exercise machine, this gut buster, sitting out there in the lounge room. It had a belt you put round your waist which vibrates really quickly. Breaks up the fat cells. A drunken wideboy locks himself in and cranks it up to full power – smoke starts billowing out of the thing and it sucks the wideboy closer and closer, into its maw. He's screaming because his arse is being torn to pieces, everyone's panicking, no one knows how to turn it off or disconnect the belt, and suddenly it vibrates itself to pieces and starts snapping and slapping like a crazed rubber snake. Somebody set fire to all the posters around the room, and while we're trying to beat out the flames, one of the Goths jumped into the next door neighbours' pool, slicing through a carpet of thick green algae on the surface. He was stark naked, white as a magician's rabbit, and had jumped from the roof. A dozen people were up there, fucked on alcohol, acid and nitrous oxide. Every now and then, you'd hear someone slide off and crash to the ground. I woke up the next morning buried in furniture.

The domestic tensions kicked into second gear pretty much the following day. I don't recall the specifics of the incident, but I think the girls had just come home from a shit day in hell when Dirk waltzed in and demanded to know where his dinner was. Jesus, I shudder to think of it. He obviously hadn't had much to do with women because I

Sarah

I lived with a cop who was also a homophobic Nazi. It was in Paddington and he was always complaining about 'filthy' gays and how they brought down the neighbourhood. The thing was, one of our other flatmates was openly gay. The cop would carry on like this around him but he never actually attacked him personally. A couple of years after I'd moved on I met the gay guy who told me that the cop and he were having an affair at the time. They used to wear his gun and police hat to bed.

don't know a single straight guy who'd dare pull a stunt like that. Not one, out of all of the arse-scratching, beer-guzzling yahoos I've lived with. Your cock would be on the chopping block before you could scream. We were still scraping bits of Dirk off the wall three days later. Crazy Nina was particularly harsh. It was a bad moon rising. Nina and Dirk were simply programmed contra to each other. She must have spotted him as the weak link in the house, because she bore down on him without mercy. They'd have furious arguments over whose turn it was to hold the TV remote, whether or not the pineapple chunks went on the third shelf or the fourth shelf in the cupboard, whether it was Tiny Teddies or Iced Vo-Vo's in the shopping trolley this week. Really bitter gouging encounters which sent Em and me into hiding to laugh ourselves sick.

There's a club out there for Crazy Nina's ex-flatmates. There must be dozens of us now. We get together occasionally, rent a hotel for speeches, dinner and drinks. Sometimes we go to the opera together. We're all bonded by having lived with her. Other people just don't understand. Nina looked normal. She was a beautiful girl, raven-haired, with striking green eyes. She knew how to present. She seemed like a competent human being. But at her core? A heart of Darkness. You didn't get to know this until you had lived with her for a while. She had a very good act. Fooled us for weeks. As I said, it's difficult to recall the details now. Only the texture and echoes remain.

Sometimes you can tell straight off that a lunatic is bearing down upon you. During the interview, when black leathery wings burst from their back and their head does the three-sixty, hosing the room down with thick, green pea soup, it's a pretty easy thing to grab the biro and scratch their name from the list. Most often, however, it takes about a week. You'll wake up at two or three in the morning to the sound of your new flatmate, the quiet librarian, ranting and screaming at her boyfriend as she stoves in the windscreen of his Volvo with a Club Lock in an attempt to stop him driving away. Or maybe you'll be rooting around in the freezer, trying to figure out how to get to the Vodka or that last fish finger, or the legendary Lost Tab of Acid, and you'll notice that the ice cube tray has been filled full of tomato paste. Or you'll catch the new girl sandpapering her books. For that fresh, just brought home look. Or you'll come home late one night and trip over a new hat stand. I've noticed that neurotic young women all own hat stands. And hats. Lots of them.

Worst-case scenario was this mad hatter called Lucy. No connection to Lucinda the Loon. She used the hat stand to keep her partner in place. He was three times her size but she bent him to her will by picking the hat stand up and bashing him with it, hats and all. You'd come home to an incredibly clean house and know there'd been a domestic, because the hats all had dents in them. She was nice before she moved in. But she turned. If she didn't get what she wanted, she'd storm around the house slamming doors, waiting for her poor boyfriend to get home. Then she'd scream like a banshee and bash him with the hat stand, the second he walked in through the door.

But on the big scale of things, Lucy the mad hatter was a rank amateur. Had her tagged as nutter within two days.

With Crazy Nina, it took time. It was a constant chafing which rubbed on your nerves, rubbed them raw in the end – little oddities and quirks gathering into a tsunami of obsessions and strangeness. She was a list fascist. It was her first law of share house dynamics. For every action, there had to be a long list of activity, drawn up by Nina. The upshot of it all was generally that everybody got jobs to do and bills to pay, except Nina, who was hard at work drafting the next list. She also experimented on kittens. Raised them inside a locked, airtight, explosively hot house on a diet of soy extract and vegetable gruel. She never cleaned up after them. They crawled inside the pile of clothes I slept under and relieved themselves at least two times a day.

I though about killing them. I've done it before. I lived with this girl, Laura. She had a pet guinea pig, called it Chester. It was a surrogate love interest. She let it sleep in a rolled-up jumper on the pillow next to her. Talked to it all of the time. While she was watching television, reading a book, playing the stereo. She even had guinea pig music on CD for Christ's sake. Debussy, I think. Anyway Laura had a real date one night. Some desperado from the office. Probably the new guy. She was clued in enough to realise the pig was a no-show for the date, and tied herself in knots over whether to go or pike out. She drove me crazy, asking what she should do. I said I'd look after it if she'd just get out of the house, and she reluctantly agreed. Left me two typed pages of instructions. Soon as she was gone, I locked Chester in the bathroom and luxuriated in my first night alone in the house. I fell asleep in front of the teev, woke up about ten o'clock. I figured I'd better let the pig out or it might go a bit shack wacky. She'd notice, believe me. So I opened the door, expecting it to bolt out between my legs, but there's no activity inside the bathroom. I called out its name. 'Chester!' Nothing. My stomach began a slow forward roll. There weren't too many places for it to hide.

Only one really. My heart was really starting to hammer as I walked over and peered in. The toilet bowl. Yep. There he was. Poor little sucker. Probably kept his head above water for a couple of hours. I threw all my shit in an overnight bag and ran for it. Sorry about that Laura.

Now where was I? Ah yes, the other loony.

Nina enmeshed the house in this fantastically complicated series of lies and abstractions by which she ordered her daily affairs. She was avoiding an ex-boyfriend who'd lent her a tape recorder and wanted it back, somebody else who'd loaned her some lecture notes and wanted them back, the Hilton Hotel where she worked when she felt like it, and her mother from whom she had inherited her personality. We had different stories for each of them. We had to tell the Hilton that she'd been in a car accident. We had to tell the people from Uni she was in Sydney. We had to tell her mother that she was at her sister's place. And of course we got it all hopelessly wrong. We told work she was in Sydney and her mother that she was in a car accident and her boyfriend that she was gay. So then we got a list explaining where we had let her down. She pinned photocopies of that one to our bedroom doors. Or the TV set in my case. It started getting way out of hand. Our neighbours, old Ted and Mavis, called Em over to their back verandah one afternoon, and whispered 'Isn't it terrible about Nina?'

'Beg pardon?' said Em.

'John, getting her pregnant, forcing her to get an

abortion. She's been crying all day.'

We made one last effort before Crazy Nina crashed and burned us completely. Told her we were going to the beach for a few days, asked her if she wanted to come. She said that sounded like a great idea. Dirk was in the bad books for some reason, so we organised the holiday behind his back. The morning of the trip, everyone had packed and was

Bill

I went to a red house-warming party where there was going to be some blackjack played. I was curious because I like to play cards and the people throwing the party knew nothing about cooking. So we all turn up wearing red. We sit down. They had red plates. They brought out this big pot of boiling water with hot dogs in it. Dumped them on a plate with a lot of tomato sauce. Then they slopped out all this beetroot. Then all this red cabbage crap. Three or four of these red horrors, then some crook red wine and red jelly. Then they started playing blackjack. There was a really weird feeling in the air so I left. I found out it had turned into strip blackjack and they all ended up fucking each other. A nightmare. It must have been all the preservatives and red shit they were eating. Drove them crazy and the genitals came out. They were probably red too.

bouncing off the walls like kids dosed up on red cordial. But Nina was sitting around in her tracksuit, eating buttered toast and looking like she wouldn't be escaping from the gravitational pull of the bean bag for three months. She has a problem. Doesn't think it's a very good idea for people who live together to spend too much time together.

She wouldn't look at us. Just stared at the TV, really drilled into *Fat Cat and Friends*. We kept at her for a while, but she said the weather would be bad, she had laundry to do, assignments to write. We had to strong-arm her into the car. After all, this was partly for her benefit. To help her chill out. And it wasn't even a total disaster – there was even one moment when she morphed back into human form for about two hours. We had a picnic up on a headland near a lighthouse. Sat on blankets in the dunes to keep out of the wind. Had beers and fried chicken, fruit, cheese and fresh bread. We were totally disconnected. It seemed to calm Nina right down. A really nice moment. But when we packed up and went back to the car, the wings burst from her back all over again. The following week, we were back at the house and she appeared in the living room, said, 'I'm just going round the shop,' walked out, and never came back. We didn't bother calling the cops. Word eventually filtered down that she had moved in with a girlfriend called Tanya.

At this stage, I'd been pulling a lot of cones with a girl called Joanne. That's my courtship ritual. Pull so many cones with a girl that we become brain dead and decide to go out together. I pulled so many with Joanne that I damaged my lungs and caught some horrible kind of chest infection. A doctor at the 24hr clinic gave me some tablets for it. I don't know whether I was allergic to the tablets or whether they reacted against the massive quantities of dope in my bloodstream, but I broke out in these amazing red welts. They were like little mesas and canyons. They started on the insides of my elbows and climbed symmetrically all over my body. Covered my face and lips. I looked like The Thing from *The Fantastic Four*. I was stripped down to my jocks, standing in front of a full length mirror to check out this freak show when there's a knock at the door and Tanya bursts in, babbling about Nina. Saying she's crazed, she's insane. I go yeah, for sure. Then Tanya notices my appearance.

'What's up with you?'

'Allergic reaction.'

And she continues without missing a beat. Crazy Nina had lobbed into her place a few days ago. Said we had thrown her out. Tanya thought that was terrible, insisted that she move in with her. Nina agrees. There are a few adjustments to be made, of course, but they're minor. Nina has to borrow Tanya's keys. The pineapple chunks have to be moved to the third shelf. Tanya has been after this very well-known lawyer for ages and Nina is cramping her style. But otherwise, it's cool. She's doing her bit for the Sisterhood. But on this particular night, Tanya gets home and the house is dark and locked up. She's given Nina her keys, and Nina has assured her that she'll be home to let her in. But she isn't. Tanya knocks on the door, sits on the front step for half an hour, and finally decides to break in. She ends up climbing the trellis under her window. Tanya is very much a silk scarf and Chanel girl, but she makes the climb, levers herself through the window and crashes to the floor. Then she freezes. There's someone in her room. This house has been burgled three times in the last two months, and the panic response is rushing through her head like a train crashing off the rails. Then she realises the intruder is in her bed. There are two of them. She turns on the light. It's crazy Nina and the lawyer. He's wearing Tanya's white cowboy boots. Madness. Tanya fled, came over to our place and went to pieces.

We fled too, in the end. The house was mondo disgusto, humming with bad vibes and settling layers of toxic effect. Nina had come back briefly to liberate the kittens, her clothes and Em's cooking pots. She put the pots into storage and sent a lawyer's letter disputing ownership. She was like a twister tearing through a trailer park after an earthquake, so we found another house up in the mountains outside town, and prepared to withdraw to a quieter life. But our phased retreat became a panic stricken rout when Crazy Nina's mother threatened to come around and sort out this cooking pot business once and for all. She had prepared a list. It would explain everything. I think I saw her car pull into the driveway as we disappeared over the hill.

Our new place was the best house I've ever lived in – polished wood floors throughout, half-way up a mountain, surrounded by sub-tropical rain forest. Em hung all this coloured cloth and shit from the ceiling, turned the place into a bedouin tent. Very cool. We got this girl in to replace Crazy Nina but she was diagnosed schizo and moved out. I just couldn't understand it. She was one of the sanest, most reasonable people I've ever met. Cooked a damn fine minestrone. Sadly when she left, domestic harmony left with her.

Dirk had been partially rehabilitated by his feud with Crazy Nina. But when the war with her was resolved, we discovered a new Dirk living amongst us. An uptight, suspicious Dirk. Nothing like the fun-loving, oddly haired, dope-smoking Dirk we had previously known. This new Dirk was always alert and on guard, because he had discovered he was gay. He trawled for homophobic intent in all our conversations and domestic arrangements. He put posters of nude, grinning men all over the kitchen because it made him feel comfortable. We took them down because we were fascists. We asked him if he wanted dinner one night and he said no, he was going out. But when he found out we had made his favourite apricot chicken, he said we tricked him into saying no. Said we probably thought being straight was better than being gay. Said we were just like Fred Nile.

Yes I know. I'm being hard. But I tried, honest I did. While I was in Sydney for some work, Dirk wrote me a note, all cut up because his parents' minds had imploded and they'd told him never to darken their doorstep again. I could see this was weighing heavily on him. His parents were a couple of Nazi pinheads, but they were his parents. Who else was going to do his laundry? So I write him a note in return, figuring it's a chance to square the ledger, a chance to strut my credentials as a broadminded guy. You know, straight man-gay man, all brothers under the skin sort of thing. I write Dirk a letter suggesting that if his parents are unable to cope with his sexual orientation, it's their problem, not his. I said if I was a gay guy, I wouldn't

Monica

I lived with two merchant bankers. One of them brought this Brazilian girl home and made her stay in the flat for four days. Kept her prisoner really. Tried to get into her pants every night. The girl only spoke French and Spanish and I had to translate. He'd get home about eleven most nights, close the lounge room door and launch another attempt on this poor girl. She came to me one night, absolutely desperate and said 'Please help me.' She didn't want to stay but he was locking her in every day. He used to ring me during the day and say 'Is that bitch still there'. I let her out and gave her twenty bucks to get to the consulate.

be worrying about my parents. I'd be getting laid every night. I mean, you're hitting on guys right? That's what I wrote him. And it didn't come easy. There was more empathy and understanding in that note than I'd ever needed in ten years of writing to girlfriends. Dirk broke down when he read it. But not from gratitude. He burst into tears, said it was typical really, and got stuck into my homophobia like a big hot meal.

So I brought Taylor the taxi driver back into my life, into all of our lives really. He'd given up the booze again. Needed a place to stay, so I offered him the spare room. I explained the whole set-up to the house before Taylor moved in, but Dirk went to pieces anyway. Said he didn't think Taylor would respect his homosexuality. Don't know why. He'd ditched the camouflage pants after he got off the grog and his main source of happiness now came from baking bread. Hundreds of loaves. You'd get home and he'd be in the kitchen wearing an apron over his Blundstones and King Gees. Hell, Dirk should have taken him on as a role model. But it didn't work out, and I've got to admit, that was kind of the plan. Relations soured and an exchange of notes began between Dirk and Taylor, culminating in Taylor plunging a huge hunting knife through a big piece of butcher's paper and into the door of Dirk's room. The message on the paper, finger-painted Charles Manson-style in pig's blood, said simply, 'You are dead meat on a hook, mate.'

Game, set and match, Taylor.

Share House Artefacts : Number Three

Bucket Bong

UNDERSTAND THE TECHNOLOGY.

A joint is simple. Just like the rollies
Grandad smoked while seeing off Rommel.
Sort of. Some of the good gear, chopped
up, rolled in between two fag papers and
smoked like a cigarette.
NOTE: YOU MUST INHALE.
A bong is more complicated, usually
a home-made device, often constructed
from a plastic Orchy bottle, a small
length of garden hose and a metallic
or alfoil-based cone.
But a bucket bong is something else again.
It relies on air pressure to shotgun a
cooler, vaster, more powerful smoke
straight into the lungs. As much more
smoke can be pushed in and held for so
much longer the Bucket has a reputation
for turning the most bogus leaf into
killer weed. It is to the simple bong as
the cruise missile is to the snide remark.

CAN YOUR HOME AFFORD TO BE WITHOUT ONE?

THE YELLOW UNDERPANTS OF ROCK'N'ROLL

I had some lesbian trouble my first time in Sydney – nothing too serious, but worth putting down on the permanent record. I was on the run, visiting my friend Scarey Bill in the middle of winter. He'd set me up on a mattress in the lounge room of the Surry Hills terrace he shared with his girlfriend and three other fringe dwellers. We went out drinking the first night and I came home really looking forward to that mattress on the floor. Figured on crawling into my sleeping bag, maybe catching some bad late night teev in front of the little log fire. Not being much of a pool player, Scarey Bill left the pub early, beat me home by an hour and fluttered off to bed because he and his girlfriend couldn't keep their hands off each other. When I finally got home, I found these two women – shaven-headed lesbians – writhing around in my sleeping bag in the 69 position. Feet sticking out of the sack and everything.

Steven

Someone gave me this drug at our housewarming. It was a heavy downer which sent me to bed in the middle of the party. I was mostly asleep when this couple came into the room. They hopped onto the bed and started thrashing about. I rolled away and tried to sleep. My head was in the corner of the room because the bed was pushed in there.
I had the small of this girl's back against the side of my face. This guy's thrusting is banging my head against the wall. I woke up and thought 'What the fuck?' Bang bang bang bang. 'Oh for fuck's sake.' I slid out from under them. But I'd woken up in this dream state, momentarily aroused. So I fucked her from the back while she was slurping on this boy. I participated for all of four minutes. Now that was a real share situation.

I figured they weren't on for a threesome so I climbed up to Scarey Bill's room but could hear the beast with two backs at work in there too. So I stood on the turn in the staircase for some time, reviewing the options. In the end I shrugged. There was a patch of carpet beneath my feet. I'd camp there. It was very late and I was very tired – I must have slept for all of four and a half minutes before I woke up freezing to death. I went down to the kitchen, collected all the tea towels I could find and tried making them into a sort of quilt. I woke up freezing again, five and a half minutes later.

I started prowling around the house, rubbing myself against anything that was even remotely warm. Being a Queenslander in the middle of a southern winter, I was desperate. It was getting on for four in the morning when I thought to run a hot bath and slip into that. Ahh yes. I remember it well. Gave me twenty minutes of blessed sleep before the water went cold and I had to top it up. I did that three or four times before the hot water ran out. Weak grey light was leaking in through the windows when I finally scratched on Scarey Bill's door and pushed my way in, crying that the lesbians had stolen my bed. Scarey and his girlfriend sat bolt upright in horror. 'That's terrible,' they said. Bill jumped up and pulled his action mackintosh off the clothes rack. A great big warm thing. Saliva actually squirted into my mouth when I saw it. I got the coat and a little patch of carpet at the foot of their bed. That coat was like heaven. If he'd only left it downstairs five hours ago, I'd have been a happy man.

Sydney at least seemed better than Melbourne. I'd torched every Brisbane bridge I could get my lighter underneath – Telecom, L.J. Hooker, Social Security, my parents, my friends and this minor league businessman I'd defamed on public radio. The process server from his law firm found me on a hot summer's day. I'd stripped back to my underwear and was sucking on a lime-green paddlepop. This guy roars up in his Porsche, bounds up the stairs and hits me with a writ. I get it into my head to be really rude to him and start mouthing off, telling him he's an ugly man, a parasite, but the thing is, the paddlepop's melting all over my hand as I give this guy a piece of my mind. My delivery is really brutal, really apt, but there's paddlepop everywhere and I'm in my undies. The guy just grins, bounds back down the stairs, hops into his Porsche and drives off. I tear the writ into tiny pieces, leave two weeks rent and leg it out of Dodge City. Ironically, so does the businessman a little bit later.

Word of mouth got me out of Bill's place and into a flat in a run-down block off Oxford Street, Darlinghurst. Real skid row. I moved in on a rainy Tuesday. Three different types of mould were vying for supremacy over the ground floor. It was like living in a huge laundry bag. Somebody had spray-painted a warning on the second floor landing – '*Don't come any closer Geoffrey. We have a gun.*'

When I first got there, these two guys had passed out in a pool of old piss in the hallway downstairs. One of them had a brown paper bag clutched to his chest. I figured it was probably a smack pack. I spent all day moving my stuff into this place. These guys lay in the hallway for hours, completely unconscious. They could have been dead except they'd wheeze or cough every now and then. One of them woke up as I was taking the last load in, opened the brown bag and started eating a cheese sandwich. I closed the door on him but about ten minutes later I came running back out because this terrible banging and screaming had started up. The other guy had regained consciousness and discovered his mate had scarfed the whole sanger, hadn't even left him a crust. They got into a terrible fight over it. Beat the living Bejesus out of each other. I learned not to open my door too much after that. The place was riddled with junkies and dealers and all sorts of lowlife. I complained to the caretaker about the lack of security and the scumbags wandering in day and night, but he didn't give a shit. The cops came for him after he squeezed off two clips from an assault rifle inside his basement flat. Amphetamine psychosis, they said. Soon as he got bail, he came back and tried to set the apartment on fire.

I had two flatmates to begin with in this place, and they started a band soon after I moved in. Suddenly the place became a band house – roadies, groupies, sycophants, band managers, sound and lighting engineers, fellow musos

Jane

I lived with a nice girl, Marina. She was a court
reporter. We had a lease on a great terrace and
just wanted a nice flatmate for the last room, but
we had dreadful trouble getting one. One guy actually moved in but he ended up wanting to go out
with Marina. She had to ditch him and look for
another one. We then interviewed a succession of
loonies. We had a Seventh Day Adventist space
cadet, a vegetarian who stressed the fact that she
didn't like to see meat in the fridge. In fact she
wanted to know had there ever been meat in this
fridge and had we ever considered replacing it on
the off-chance. She was standing on the patio ripping Marina's geraniums to shreds as she was saying
this. Marina stood glaring at the leaves as they
were pulled to pieces. Then we interviewed some guy
who checked the tide, a meteorologist or something.
We put the trick question to him 'What about   >

and weirdoes would drop by at all hours. At first it had been
just Hooper, Tammy and me. Then Jeremy moved in from
this fibro cottage he'd been renting over in Redfern. Jeremy
was running away from a psychotic housemate, a hyper-
violent invalid pensioner. This guy was a real counter
jumper. If the Powerful Ones even hinted at hassling him
down at Darlinghurst DSS, he'd go sub-orbital, jump the

> parties?' and he thought that was an invita-
tion. He said 'Oh I love parties, the bigger the
better. I'm a party animal. I'm on for one any
time.' We interviewed this older guy who said he
didn't actually want to live there. He just needed
an address to give his wife's lawyers. A French
backpacker who sat himself down in front of the
television, asked for a TV guide and just would
not leave. A hippy who was looking for somewhere
to find himself.
Then Siimon arrived in his cheap Adidas sprint
shoes, jeans and checked shirt. He hammered on the
floor to check whether it would support his king-
size water bed. When he'd ascertained his boudoir
could make it he proceeded to tell us he went to
the Sydney. We're going the Sydney What? And he
goes Sydney Uni. He was studying part-time to be
an accountant. I asked him what he did with the
rest of his time and he became a bit sheepish. He
said he worked. We asked where and he knew the >

counter and start screeching like a Gila monster with
Tourette's Syndrome. He was useful if you had your own
hassles with the dole fascists, because you could take him
along and when they saw you together they'd process the
hell out of you in less than three minutes. But on balance,
he just wasn't worth it. So Jeremy packed a bag one night
and slipped away. Refused to leave our house for three

> gig was up. He asked us if we'd ever heard of
Studs Incorporated. I was scratching my head
thinking, 'God I know that name.' And Marina's
going, 'Is it a restaurant?'
I said, 'Oh it's a gay paper isn't it? A
magazine?' And he was like, 'No no no no no ...
it's uhm it's ... strippers.'
I went, ' ... Oh. Male strippers?' and he blathered
on that they had women too. He was their manager
and he'd taken them to new heights. It was a
hands-on thing. You know. For the accounting
degree. He stressed they were all heterosexual so
there was nothing to be worried about. We had
visions of them all coming home for coffee and
trying their hands-on thing with us. Marina started writing down his name and he says, 'That's
Siimon with two 'i's thanks'. And she goes, 'Right
Siimon with two 'i's we'll give you a call' and
threw the piece of paper over her shoulder into
the bin.

weeks in case this guy saw him on the street.

Jeremy was perennially three subjects short of a law
degree and loved to sue people. In the short time I knew
him he must have had about three lawsuits running. One
with a former employer, another with some neighbour from
Redfern, and one with a cabbie who refused to accept
American dollars for a fair. This Lebanese character had

picked him up in the Cross late one night on the tail-end jag of a two month backpacking jaunt through the States. I remember waking to shouts in the street and the sound of Jeremy running into the flat and slamming the door. He'd tried to explain to the cabbie in his excitable Sydney Grammar way that because of the 'i-n-t-e-r-n-a-shhh-nl eggschange rate', the driver would actually be making a profit on the crumpled greenbacks he'd thrust into his face. But the cabbie chased Jeremy with a Club Lock, yelling abuse in his native tongue. In the cold, hard light of day, Jeremy decided the only course of action was to relentlessly pursue the poor bastard through the courts for assault.

Apart from his flourishing legal practice, Jeremy had a bass guitar and a lot of time on his hands. That was the catalyst for our house to form a band. Hooper and Jeremy put the band together with Keith, the polite drummer who moved in downstairs and practiced on icecream buckets and sheets of foolscap instead of his $7,000 Ludwig drum kit, because he was a quiet kind of guy and didn't want to put anyone out. Keith was a locum at Prince of Wales Hospital and the house became a drop-in centre for tired-looking residents in the dead zone between shifts. These residents used to work incredibly long hours each day, and Keith and his friend Nobby used to take speed or a speed-like drug called Duromin, to keep themselves awake for work. Unfortunately, it soon spilled over into their private lives. I remember getting up for work at 7.30am just in time to see Keith and Nobby – who's now a plastic surgeon or something – running around the house in yesterday's clothes, biting and tearing at each other in an excited frenzy to get into the kitchen and eat the little cubes of frozen tomato paste they had put in the ice tray in the fridge.

There's no privacy in a band house. No respect for boundaries or personal space. If you want privacy, you go out. If you want respect, you move out. I discovered this after making my first significant furniture purchase since the Foster-Lindburgh incident. I bought this wild 1920's walnut veneer dining suite from an antique dealer. Moved it in the Wednesday the Bad Seeds played the Dark Coma. I wasn't going to the concert – can't stand Nick Cave – but I scammed my girlfriend Sweden and the house band onto the door list because I was writing for *Rolling Stone* at the time, and they'd kick me back some tickets when they didn't have the cash to pay me up front. The night of the concert, I went to bed early. It was freezing cold, pissing down rain and everyone but me was on all sorts of weird drugs. The household got out of this concert ripped off their heads and came back to the flat. They didn't care about anything, these people. One of the house band's dopey roadies took off his big thick slopping wet cable-knit jumper, and sat down on one of my antique walnut-veneer dining suite chairs. His string singlet was wet, his body temperature was racing and he basically steamed my chair.

He wandered off in the wee hours of the morning and I came out the next day to find the wreckage in my living room. What had been this lovely, nutty-brown, tiger-skin sheen was now a weird kind of misty grey lattice work maze. Like it had been spray-painted. I took it back to the shop and they couldn't believe it. A week hadn't passed and I had fucked this beautiful piece of furniture which had survived since the 1920's.

The band of course was completely hopeless. Called themselves The Black Dogs. I tagged along with them on a three week death march to a terminal point in Mt Isa, where they'd landed a semi-permanent gig at the Overland Hotel. *Rolling Stone* came up with the idea. Said they wanted a gritty account of a pub rock band on the road, and in a Duromin delirium I came up with this great concept piece. I'd call the article *The Yellow Underpants of Rock 'n' Roll*, get the Lizard Man, the band's frightening lead singer, to buy a pair of white Calvin Klein boxer shorts on the first day of the tour, and get him to wear the underpants consistently for six weeks on the road. (This was a not a big ask given Milo's unwashed jeans-wearing record at King Street.) We'd take a photo of the Lizard Man's underpants at the end of the tour and I would somehow convince the editor to run it as a front cover. I don't remember the rationale for all this, but I do recall that the phrase *The Yellow Underpants of Rock 'n' Roll* evolved into a short-hand tag for any unsavoury truth about the nature of the music industry. Like the set-up at the Overland in Mt. Isa, for example. The Overland payed the band a handful of beer-soaked dollars to play every night, and threw in free accommodation at a house across the road. The house had two pool tables downstairs, which wasn't too bad, but it was the only place in Mt Isa that didn't have air-conditioning. There were a couple of ceiling fans but they were fucked from having had so much stuff thrown into them. The heat was unbearable. We couldn't stand it, so we'd go to the pub, spend our handful of cash on beer, running up debt, paying it off, and running it up again. The other problem was those locals who thought it was hip to come back after the gig and have drinks in the house because you were a band. You'd get back and there'd be about thirty rednecks drinking in your lounge room, wheeling out the bullshit.

They'd been into this ritual for years. Everyone knew each other in Mt Isa, so you had all these bullshit artists who couldn't bullshit each other any more. They'd sit around waiting for the next band to roll into town – strangers who didn't know them. Then you'd get the racing car drivers, the hang gliders, the croc wrestlers and mercenaries all coming out of the woodwork to tell you about their fascinating lives. We took it for a few days before turning feral. We'd go, 'Yeah, yeah, yeah,' and piss off to our rooms, but it wouldn't bother them – they'd hang around, keeping the bullshit flowing until the early hours of the morning.

Michael

Alan was the Sega player from Hell. He decided he
didn't like living at his own place so he was
always coming around and visiting Roy, my flatmate.
They'd pull a dozen cones then Alan would attach
the Sega to the telly. We only had one TV, mine. So
he just moved in and turned the place into a video
game parlour. He'd play games for six or seven
hours at a time. Wouldn't matter whether it was
night or day. He'd play for a whole day, pull a few
cones, eat some delivery food, play for a night,
crash on our couch, wake up and start playing
again. I don't know how he did it. Occasionally
he'd go off to a couple of classes during the day.
Then he'd come back and plug in the Sega. He only
stopped after three or four months when his girl
friend dropped him. He was really surprised at her.

We did our best to get picked up by the local
women who'd have quiet beds and air conditioning. It was
a desperation thing. I went off with a dancing girl who
shuffled around in a cage when the DJ was on between sets.
She had air-con and a car, which Hooper and I tooled
around in while she was at work. But there was a price to
be paid for all that of course – hard blown, mining town
sex.

It was the women torched the tour in the end. Hooper, who played quiet guitar or something, ended up as a kind of tragic trophy for a particularly hard-faced specimen. He spat the dummy, loaded the band's yellow van with as much equipment as he could steal from the pub and drove into a tree. There was some kind of police inquiry and the whole yellow underpants trip started to get very ugly. We had to hitch back to Brisbane. Keith was so upset he sold his drum kit to pay for an airline ticket out of there, flew straight back to Sydney. He'd moved out by the time I got home. I still see him occasionally, walking up Victoria Street. I've tried chatting with him but you can see the whole thing is scar tissue now.

Jeremy turned into an incredible band Nazi in Brisbane, thought he could salvage the whole disaster by organising a couple of gigs and even went so far as to recruit my old school friend Stuart to fill in on drums. Jeremy had gone insane by this stage. He was completely disconnected from the local scene but he monstered every half-smart operator in town until he got a couple of dates. There was real madness about the week The Black Dogs were in Brisbane.

I'd run out of lounge room floors to crash on in Brisbane, so in desperation I rang my parents and asked if I could stay with them. Then Jeremy told me that he and Hooper had enough money for a motel but I'd have to do the right thing by the Lizard Man. Put him up somewhere. Keep him away from them because his underpants were really beginning to smell. He had locked into this idea and refused to let go. Just would not change those underpants. I parked the Lizard Man at my parents' house and the ugliness inflated like a life raft in the back of a Japanese car.

The Lizard Man was a six-foot-two love machine who oozed really creepy sex – he had this thing about being naked, couldn't wait to get his gear off and run his hands up and down his body. He had really bad skin on his back. Weeping sores and blisters, big black bristling hairs that stuck out from his neck and shoulders like spider legs. And of course there was the underpants thing. He'd gone mad for it. Really wanted his soiled Calvin's on the cover of *Rolling Stone*. He stuck to me like glue.

We got to my parents' house and it all got too hard. I'd signed on for the Isa tour as a straight-forward working holiday – a Hemingway trip, like running the bulls or killing a marlin. Plenty of blood, but at the end of the day you put the book down and crawl between the clean sheets. Now, here we were. The Lizard Man and I. At home with my parents in Stafford.

In a weird kind of way he did himself credit by not even attempting to deviate from the script while he was

Jon

The new flatmate arrived with a dog. It was skinny, it had fleas and it dribbled a lot. A vote was
taken and it was decided that the dog was NOT to
be allowed inside. The dog-owner agreed, although
it soon became obvious that he was letting the dog
inside when everyone else was out. The house
became infested with fleas. The other flatmates
took it very well, they were an easy-going bunch.
In fact they began Flea Races in which they would
put on only a pair of shorts, and run through the
house to see how few fleas they could pick up. The
record was 12. This, remember, was full-speed running right through the centre corridor of a
Queenslander. The fleas were difficult to tally
because they kept jumping around while you were
trying to count them.

around them. Took it all in his stride, explained to me later
that he didn't want to be unnatural. So he got around with
his shirt off, practiced his saxophone loudly in the living
room, even jerked off in the shower.

The pressure was there from day one. A migraine
which just wouldn't quit. My parents, decent folk who
didn't deserve this, started locking themselves in their
bedroom. I tried to do the right thing. Kept the Lizard Man

out of the house as long as I could. We trawled through a lot of pubs and parties, searching for some poor stupid girl I could dump him on. But no. The night we had some interest from a couple of Gold Coast hairdressers, both off their tits on ecstasy, the Lizard Man sidled up to me and asked, in a really reasonable tone, if I thought my parents would mind him fucking them both on the lounge room floor. 'It's two in the morning,' he said. 'I'd be really quiet. I'll have them out of there the second I'm done.'

I lost it. Cabbed it over to Jeremy's room at the Travelodge. Found Hooper and him carousing with a couple of girls who said they were from *Paradise Beach*. Told them the article was dead, the band was doomed and I was going back to Sydney. They weren't really surprised. The yellow underpants of rock 'n roll? – I was wearing them, and I don't even like music.

I headed back to my parent's place, grimly determined to pack my bags, throw the Lizard Man out and spend the next few years redeeming myself in their eyes. My Dad, the quiet man, was waiting for me. My Dad really only speaks when he has something important to say, and this time it was, *'Get this idiot out of my house'*. I nodded wearily and started to say I'd take care of it all when I saw a terrible thing out of the corner of my eye. Over my father's shoulder, out of his field of view, I could see the Lizard Man peeling out of his clothes and walking up the stairs in the nude. Leaving his gear in a pile on the floor.

He'd wanted a shower and was just being *natural* about it. Walked all the way up to the bathroom, naked, as he would have at home. The sight of his weeping, bristly back and acned bottom disappearing up the stairs was too much. My brain locked up like the brakes of a speeding car. It was a turning point in my life. A Satan's lounge room goat's head moment. I was never going to have this sort of trouble again. It was insane. It was madness. Real people don't behave like this. Real people have jobs and families and live in clean houses and drive cars that work, and they do the shopping, and their fridges are full of fresh food and their clothes are washed and clean and ready for the first day of the rest of their lives. Naked love monsters don't prowl through their houses, practicing the sax and wondering if it would be all right to fuck a couple of hairdressers on the floor. It just doesn't happen.

My parents and I did speak to each other again. Eventually. After about two years. But we never mention the Lizard Man.

Voices of the Damned

Pete

ON BEING A FLATMATE FROM HELL.

Musical taste is one of the great
sleeping issues of many share houses.
It can rival the unwashed frypan as a
source of tension.

The second or third thing you should
ask any potential flatmate is: What
sort of music do you like? A John
Denver fan just will not fit in with a
house full of Sonic Youth fanatics.

PETE IS THE GRAPHIC
DESIGNER WHO LAID OUT
THIS BOOK.

My parents set me up with the first flatmate I ever had. He was a Lismore guy who had gone to Sydney to work for the RTA. His name was Neville and he was a true career public servant. At 18 he had a brain dead job, an airless, boxy flat, some cane furniture and a disgracefully cheap stereo. He had it all, but he felt a bit lonely and thought it might be time to find a girl - the right sort of girl, you understand - and settle down, get married and breed. So he joined the local Lions Club, and went on the prowl. He urged me to do the same but I declined. Sure enough, within six weeks the first prospect was led home. I don't remember much about her, but she lasted about three weeks. Within a month the second prospect came over. Her name was Bernadette, and she was a stayer.

I was the flatmate from hell for him. I used his stereo till it broke and I ruined his candle-lit dinners. I was still into heavy metal at the time. It was my first year in Sydney. These guys I knew who were repeating senior came down from Lismore on the overnight train to catch a big Iron Maiden concert. If you were a Lismore teenager into Heavy Metal it was a big fucking deal. We had all these joints rolled up and we were completely metalled out, wearing cut-off denim jackets with 200 patches on them, wrist bands with studs all over them, replica motorcycle boots, hair everywhere, the lot. I do remember being a bit perplexed at the actual gig - it was kind of odd, you know, grown men in spandex pants and beer guts waving their fists at the audience, but we managed to get totally wasted and have a good time regardless.

Eventually the concert ended and we all decided to go over to my place to smoke the remaining joints and drink the emergency supply of beer one of the guys had thoughtfully stashed in the fridge. We staggered home, desperately stoned, only to find my quiet flatmate Neville there. Having the big Romantic Dinner with Bernadette. Her parents had even come around to be introduced to their prospective son-in-law. They'd negotiated dinner and were finishing up with coffee and chocolate mints when we stormed in, stinking of dope and beer, looking like extras from some woeful Viking movie, taking up all the space in this flat. We were confronted by these aghast middle-aged boring fart parents, this frizzy-haired girl and Neville the mustached public servant in the lemon yellow short sleeve shirt with the palm tree on the pocket, grey slacks and a cloth belt. There was an awkward moment while he introduced the parents to us. I remember looking at these

people and thinking 'Fuck, they're from
Mars.' I was becoming more and more fixated
on the lapels of the father's jacket and was
just about to reach out and inspect them
closely when they all fled to a coffee shop
on the other side of town.
Neville got away with it though. He married
her.

DON'T COME ANY CLOSER FRANKIE, WE HAVE A GUN

Dylan was a telecommunications engineer who liked to load up on acid and walk around Kings Cross taking photographs. When I met him Dylan had lived at Kippax Street for three and a half years, and had eaten at home only once in that time. His bedroom was a bat cave, completely black. He'd taped thick black cardboard over the windows and covered the walls and ceiling with Beasts of Bourbon, and Bauhaus posters. That room was a fortress of solitude. He pulled at least six cones in there every day. He'd saved twenty thousand dollars to travel around the world, but had a lot of trouble overcoming the natural inertia of all bat cave dwellers. So his other plan for spending the money was to waste an entire year getting stoned and lying on the brown couch at Kippax St. In the end it was only the promise of new and exotic drugs in Amsterdam which pulled him up off the torn cushions and out the front door. His departure set off a series of share house explosions, both conventional and nuclear, which culminated in Jeffrey the junkie turning up his toes on my green bean bag. The fate of most places I've lived tended to be tied to a core of flatmates who set up the house, defined its character, then crashed and burned as a single unit. But for two years at Kippax Street I bore witness to an unceasing procession of share house flotsam and jetsam, randomly washed up then borne away by the shifting tides of the inner city.

I say 'my house' because I stayed there – I was exhausted and out of gas. It was that same sort of movement had fucked me. Coming in and going out it made no difference at all. It all went through you like a bad wind, leaving you bare and dry and exposed. I moved into the small room at Kippax and sat out the turn of the decade; a non-contributor with eyes of glass and the heart of a tape recorder archiving the lives of those people who drifted on the tides and those who went down with the undertow.

People like Harry the doctor, who worked at the

hospital up the road and had the keys to the medicine cabinet. The house was awash with terrible drugs while he lived there but he took off on a world trip three weeks after I arrived, and I don't actually remember what he looks like, because that whole period is just a narcotic blur.

Or Kim the vet, who took Harry's room, and

Rachel

I lived with a very strange girl whose job was abolished but she simply refused to leave. I didn't know this. I had to meet her in town once and she said, 'Meet me at my office.' So I get there and she's sitting at the desk where she'd always sat. It's six o'clock, everyone had gone home. I said something about her job and she said, 'I haven't worked here since December.' About five months before. She just kept turning up. They didn't pay her, didn't try to keep her out. She just turned up and worked. When she finally tried to claim unemployment benefits the dole fascists turned up in her office and asked what she was playing at. She tried to explain that she came to work but didn't get paid. They had a lot of trouble coming to terms with that and wouldn't give her the money. She couldn't pay the rent anymore and had to move home. She's still at that office.

brought home a baby possum, which had lost its mother and fallen out of a tree. It was supposed to be cute, but it looked like a little rat and had razor-sharp claws. It tore around the house, jumping from armchair to armchair at Warp Factor 5, which really freaked out the acid heads.

Or Meredith, the cellist with the Sydney Symphony, who only had her room for a week and never actually moved in, deciding after a few days of not being there that she hated the place anyway, so she took off, leaving the room to Melissa, the big-breasted doe-eyed smack slut who loved to bellow along with Barbara Streisand records. We didn't know about the smack when we took her in, didn't actually figure it out until long after she'd left and we had to clean out her room. At first we thought all the bent spoons came from too many tubs of frozen Homer Hudson, but the 1ml syringes with the bright orange caps sealed the deal.

Melissa put herself through university by wholesaling tabs of acid and ecstacy. She sub-contracted various flatmates as distributors, giving them one freebie tab for each ten sold. We had so much acid in our freezer that when it froze over, as it invariably did, the Legend of the Lost Tab took hold with enough force to inspire expeditions deep into the freezer, eighteen months after she had left.

'I'm telling you Johnny, it's in there, I've seen a map.'

And Melissa, of course, ran The Great Credit Scam out of Kippax Street. Her first week in, she asked us if we'd mind her friend plugging a phone into our spare outlet. He wanted to move his business down from Brisbane and needed the answering machine for a week or two. Said he'd give us a television if we helped out.

Greed triumphed over suspicion, as it will, and we let him have the connection for a week before I ripped the machine out of the wall, acting on a gut instinct that something else was at work behind the bland message on the tape recorder. We never saw our TV, and never heard of the guy again, but it was too late. Melissa and her sports-jacketed American drug buddy, Carlisle, had established an ID through the phone account and used it to broker a line of credit which snaked back on us a year later when the repo men came knocking. Pretty far-sighted for a junkie, I reckon. They'd set the scam up so well, we never even suspected Melissa was behind it. One of her dopey blonde friends let the truth slip at a party, abruptly accounting for two years of confused aggravation and subterfuge.

It was kind of uncool for Melissa to pull that stunt, but she wasn't a bad girl. Even when we tumbled to the scam we couldn't forget that she'd stolen food for us and always contributed generously to the house stash, which is beyond rare in junkies. It's completely unknown. If Melissa had one black mark on her flatmate report card it was her horror boyfriend, Frankie. You might remember Frankie as the guy who made off with my CD's and fed me a line about some nightclubbing Japanese photographer at Kinselas having them. After he cleaned out my desk I rang his mother to say I was looking for him, and she asked, in this real tired voice, what had he done this time. I told her. She said she was sorry, but I'd never see those discs again. Said he'd cleaned out her Elvis collection years ago.

Before he met Melissa, Frankie went out with a girl called Ingrid, whom I vaguely knew through the Brisbane scene. He went out with her for two or three years, never letting on that he was a junkie. She moved down to Sydney with him, into this little flat at Bondi. They were both on the dole and he sold her this great story –'Let's live on your dole, pay the rent and buy food with it, and we'll save up all of my dole and go back to South Africa where my parents are rich, and we'll have a great time,'– and she believed him. He lived off her for months, shooting his dole money up his arm. Ingrid didn't tumble to his habit, until she was wearing his leather jacket one day and found all these dirty fits in the pocket. She freaked. He gave her a line about them being someone else's – he was just getting rid of them – and she believed him. They finally broke up after she walked in on him receiving a blow job in the kitchen from this transsexual who lived next door.

Frankie's name varied a bit. It was Frankie, or it was George, or maybe Anthony. And his surname was Mallory or it was Leigh or it was Jones. He'd pluck a random combination of assumed names out of the air when he introduced himself to a stranger, and if you called him the wrong name in front of them, he'd glare at you with these cold, dead eyes.

The girls all hated him. I was the only guy there at that time, and when I was away, he'd start roaming the house. The girls would be napping in their bedrooms and wake up to find Frankie grinning wetly at the end of the bed. We lost Amy the wonderbabe that way. She was a Kiwi and one of the best flatmates I ever had at Kippax. Baked great biscuits and occasionally brought home food from the restaurant where she worked — not to the same extent as Melissa, but enough to keep us away from the Krishnas. She just got tired of waking up and finding Frankie drooling at her from the end of her bed, so she moved out.

He had powerful magic. You could tell when he was in the house. His presence would settle over you about four metres from the front door, like an evil invisible mist seeping out of a crack in the footpath. We'd be interviewing potential flatmates to replace the ones he'd frightened away, when he'd appear in the lounge room, wearing only a towel. He'd be running on weird chemicals, showing off the violent tattoos and track marks on his arms, staring blankly at the newcomers and asking questions like, 'Have you ever been a communist?' Or sometimes he'd just head them off at the front patio by sitting out there in his towel, drinking beer from the bottle and burping loudly at anyone who

Kevin

I moved into this big house with a guy who moved all of his stuff into his bedroom by simply throwing it through the bedroom door. At intervals he'd straighten his room up by opening the door and throwing everything out into the lounge room. Then he'd get tired of it all and forget about it. So for two days we'd have his bedroom all over the lounge room. Then everyone would get tired of that so we'd throw it back in. He never complained. We never complained. Nothing ever happened. It just went on.

ventured in through the front gate. My CD collection disappeared because Melissa pissed off to the States with Carlisle, and Frankie had to raise the price of a bus fare back to the Gold Coast. I was pissed off at the time, but looking back, I think the loss was acceptable – it got Frankie out of the house and out of our lives forever.

Melissa was replaced by Duffy, a computer programmer, who loved to cook fried eggs. Seemed to live on them. He worked nights, got home about three in the morning, and started wolfing down fried eggs and drugs. He'd been taking acid since he was twelve. He had a rough head but a good heart, and a babe for a girlfriend – Wendy, the lead singer with a terrible northern beaches band called Wet Leather. Wendy would bring the band back to our place sometimes. They looked like off-duty police constables. Short hair and thick necks poured into short-sleeved patterned shirts and acid-wash denim.

Wendy fell in love with the bass player of the band – as the script required her to – sending Duffy off on a three week drug binge. She came back and all was forgiven, but she lost a lot of credibility a bit later when we discovered a picture of her in *People* magazine, sitting on a bed next to Ignatius Jones, a couple of lamb chops and T-bones strategically positioned over her rude bits. It was very odd. Perplexed as we were, we just couldn't quite bring ourselves to broach the subject with either Wendy or Duffy, and in the end we lost our chance. They moved into a little Glebe love shack together. Never saw them again.

We had some trouble getting people in for a while, had one of those slack periods on the flow chart. We eventually took in this Dutch guy, who turned up for an interview and pretty much refused to leave. We caved in and gave him a room, but he moved out after a few weeks, because he was dating some barmaid from the Royal Hotel and it got complicated. Or something. We covered his rent by taking in Giovanna, the young sister of a friend who wanted to see what share housing was like. She came, she saw and she moved straight home again, to be replaced by some guy known only as Mosman. I never actually met him, and nobody remembers his name. He was just some North Shore mother's boy – moved in for three days, couldn't hack it, and moved out in the dead of night.

We turned his room over to Jimbo.

Jimbo came from the bush. He was, like most country boys, a full disclosure man. Couldn't wait to get back from a date to tell the whole house about it in exacting gynaecological detail. He was an alleged handyman who destroyed everything he touched. Two months after we let him fix the bathroom, the pipes burst and the chipboard flooring he put in under this bath he installed simply rotted away. Incredibly, Jimbo didn't move out after that. He stayed and he fixed things. I ended up moving into the master bedroom with one of the girls and we put the small room on the market to help pay for the damage.

Veronica the proto-hippy took the room. She was about thirty-three, and thus too young to be an actual hippy, but she tried hard. Only cooked in earthenware pots. Stacked a lot of leaves and twigs and foul-smelling herbal teas around the kitchen. Her friends were all dream analysts and numerologists and the boys who followed her home and sat on the brown couch staring lust-eyed at her all had this wet, kind of limp look about them. Veronica, on the other hand, was the house Woman of Iron, an Aiki-jutsu black belt. Whenever we had any trouble, we'd deploy her to maintain peace through superior firepower. If only she'd been there when Frankie was around. She would have expelled him from the foot of her bed with the shattered bones of his forearms jutting out through ripped skin and muscle fibre. Don't exactly recall why Veronica moved out.

Maybe she'd just done her tour of duty, got the points up, was flying back to the real world.

Jonathan, who moved in around about then, was a very beautiful, androgynous Eurasian guy who fooled everyone during his interview. His precise way of speaking and polished manners masked an intellectual shortfall, which manifested itself in a limited conversational range: hair care products and models he had slept with. Jonathan was a totally het pork-swordsman, but he worked in a gay cafe and after he arrived we found ourselves fending off phone calls from a gaggle of increasingly desperate and ticked-off homosexuals. One even offered to fly him to New York and set him up in a photographic studio. Jonathan moved on after disgracing himself with Sara the teenage sculptor who moved in downstairs and slept through her clock radio every fucking morning. The noise blasted the whole house awake but you couldn't get her to turn it down. In the end, the only thing to do was beat the clock, get up first, sit in the living room and check out the grey-lipped horror on the faces of the hungover boys who'd stagger out of her room with their hands pressed over their bleeding ear drums. After Jonathan staggered out of her room one morning, their cred rating dipped, they moved out and Downstairs Ivan moved in.

Downstairs wore a beret and goatee, but not during his interview or we'd have set the dogs on him. He told us he was a physio, which was odd because he was a actually a successful restaurateur. He'd established a very famous bistro in Double Bay and sold it for elephant bucks a few months before he moved into our place. This raised some interesting questions in my mind – like, why lie about the physio? Why move into a dump like Kippax Street when you've got all that money? Why sit around all day in a white dressing gown watching video replays of boxing matches? Why the goatee and the beret?

Uptight Martin came in the same time as Downstairs Ivan and left within a week of his departure. Downstairs once asked me if I thought Uptight might be uptight because he was a little bit gay and didn't know it yet. It was pretty perceptive of Downstairs, who wasn't otherwise noted for his sensitivity in these matters. Uptight was a very fit man. Swam two hundred miles a week, did karate four nights, weight training the remaining three. Uptight was burning up an awful lot of nervous energy with his relentless fitness regimen, but there was not a lot of action on the babe front for a guy who was pretty good-looking and so very, very fit. I guess that could be explained by the fact that he was kind of uptight, a bit of a dick, and the babes would run a mile the first time he opened his mouth. But he'd follow Downstairs around like an abandoned puppy the whole time he lived there. And he never once complained about his own abysmal record with the ladies. Suspicious? I thought so. The only thing to do was take matters into my own hands.

I was managing an office for a couple of gay guys up on Oxford Street about that time, so when Mardi Gras came around, I made sure Uptight got a good window seat in our room to watch the parade. He thought that was just great. Kept remarking excitedly that you had to admit the guys were, you know, very fit. You just had to admit that, didn't you. I figured to score myself some brownie points by turning him over to Henner, my unattached gay boss, but before I could get this cunning plan into place,

Doug

We didn't have a laundry basket so we acquired a rogue shopping trolley. We put it on the verandah and lobbed clothes in for a few weeks. Nobody washed them of course. Then the cat moved into it. Some drunks fell asleep in it. It was there with the same load of laundry for a year. When we moved we took it down the back yard, soaked it in metho and burned the lot.

Downstairs Ivan was steamrollered by Gina and Veronica's Kippax Street bitchkrieg and moved out. Uptight followed him three days later. A great loss to Oxford Street.

Downstairs and Uptight were replaced by Paul the quiet journalist and Homer the air traffic controller. Paul was completely unremarkable, except for an ability to drink beer and play snooker for three and a half days without sleep. A credit to the profession. Homer the air traffic controller was a throwback to Derek the bank clerk, a man so tight with a dollar he had to be surgically separated from it come bill-paying time. Homer's portion of the bills was always calculated to the third decimal place, factored through some complicated algorithm which pro-rated Homer's share against whether he bought any toilet paper during the week and then how many sheets on average each person used per wipe and whether they left their bedroom lights on all night or bought any milk, and if they did buy milk did they drink only their fair share of it or were they secretly sneaking into the kitchen after bedtime for

Julia

I lived with a couple of gay boys who went a bit crazy over cleaning. This is my place right. I have the lease. These guys were always on my case saying that there were scuff marks on the floor in the kitchen and so on. One of them flipped once and was digging his finger like virtually into my throat screeching about some mark on the sink and how there were no scratchy clean towels in the house. They liked rough scratchy clean bath towels. Had to have them. They would never take me on individually. They'd take a corner each and yell at me. When I threw them out they pinched all of my Weetbix and toothpaste and scratchy clean towels.

unauthorised Milo raids? And so on and so on until your head fell to pieces, like a chocolate orange. If I'd had the money I would have paid all his bills to avoid the fortnightly mathematics.

After coming to terms with the massive telephone bill Downstairs left us, we decided to cram a foreigner into the small room out the back. Yoko San. Everybody had heard my Satomi Tiger stories and thought it might be interesting to live with someone who didn't speak the language, understand the customs, eat the food or comprehend the finances of the house. That and the whole Keating push into Asia thing. Thought we'd better have a piece of that. Yoko San lasted about three weeks. She vacuumed her room three times a day. She just didn't belong.

My old school friend Matthew was passing through Sydney about that time and I made the mistake of letting him take up the spare room. Throuble was, Matthew had a fatal character flaw. He became a floundering idiot within ten feet of any available woman. One moment you'd be talking to Matthew the rakish, devil-may-care kind of guy, and the next he'd be struck dumb because a girl had walked into the room. I spent the best part of that summer organising cocktail parties at the house in the vague hope that he might stumble across some girl, cheer up and fuck off.

Eventually he did. Her name was Fiona, and she was the painfully shy younger sister of Tracy, an old girlfriend who cut my clothes to bits the day we broke up. It was an awkward thing — I was still quite scared of Tracy when Matthew got together with her little sister at one of our costume parties. They both came as ghosts and ended up pashing off under a tangle of white sheets on the road in front of the house. It got worse. They fell hopelessly in love and Fiona then came to visit three, maybe four times a day. She and Matthew would sit on the brown couch when the rest of us were trying to watch teev, holding hands and staring into each others' eyes.

'I love you Matthew.'

'I love you Fiona.'

'I *really* love you Matthew.'

'Oh, I *really* love you Fiona.'

So I threw him out. My old school friend and everything. There is no sentiment in share housing, only mercenary self interest. And if only my self interest had been running a little stronger we might never have taken in our next flatmate. Jeffrey the junkie.

Milk Crate

HAVING TROUBLE WITH CUPBOARD SPACE?

Bottom fallen out of your shopping bag? Stairs fallen off the back of your house? Annoying isn't it.

YOU NEED TO STEAL SOME PLASTIC MILK CRATES.

These versatile by-products of the Space Program convert easily to a Bookshelf, Laundry Hamper, Futon Base, Coffee Table, Bong Stand, Foot Rest or Filing Cabinet.

PLASTIC MILK CRATES.
A THOUSAND PRACTICAL USES.

COMING FROM A FOOTPATH NEAR YOU.

DON'T COME ANY
CLOSER FRANKIE,
WE HAVE A GUN

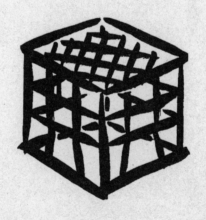

DON'T COME ANY   201
CLOSER FRANKIE,
WE HAVE A GUN

10

MOVING ON

It's funny how everyone seems to work in the sex industry these days. A couple of years ago you could guarantee that anyone in a share house was scamming social security or working a restaurant or both. But now it's the sex trade. My friend Brett has lived with two table-top dancers, a prostitute and a guy who drives prostitutes to their clients. All in the last eighteen months. Reckons it'll cost you a hundred bucks just to have a girl driven to your front door, but I don't know about that. Sounds a bit much to me.

It could be a Melbourne thing. My friend Roscoe shared a house with a B&D mistress while he was living in

Melbourne. Said she and her driver Stan came home one day, weeping with laughter. They'd been doing a job at the home of a very prominent MP. The guy's bag was to get down to handcuffs and rubber nappies and be locked in a cupboard. No sex, no contact. Just that dark, musty cupboard. He always booked for Sunday morning when the family were at church. Anyway on this particular morning one of the kids takes sick and they come home early. When Miss Donna raps on the cupboard door and tells this guy, he starts bouncing around inside, desperate to get out. They're yelling at him to calm down, they can't get the key in the lock with him thrashing about and shaking the cupboard, but that just makes it worse and after three massive thuds the cupboard rocks and teeters on the edge of balance, then falls forward, crashing face down on the carpet. Uh oh. Stan thinks quickly, stomps an air hole in the back and then flees with Miss Donna, passing the stunned family members on the front steps.

You can see this guy every now and then making a speech about the importance of supporting the traditional family.

I guess it's got something to do with Melbourne being a very English sort of town, a lot of private boarding schools inculcating a fondness for cold showers and birch-bark floggings amongst the ruling classes. It's an uptight place, incredibly constipated on issues of form. As a general rule in any city you wouldn't want to move in with somebody who actually owns the house. Chances are they won't appreciate you playing corridor golf or stripping down your hog in the lounge room. But that general injunction becomes an iron law in Melbourne.

Always be wary of phrases like, 'My house is your house. Feel comfortable. Feel free to use all the facilities. Just treat it like your home.' If you hear those phrases, run, don't look back, don't stop or turn, just run. What happens is that people buy these houses and can't make the payments so they get someone in. This woman I know, this older woman, let's call her Celine, went through a very exclusive agency and found this nice place in East Melbourne. The owner was an older guy doing the place up, needed someone to share.

If she'd sussed the garage when she first moved in she might have had an idea of what was in store. It was all there. His whole personality. Screws, nails, hammers, chisels, saws, everything hanging up or put away in little containers, all carefully graded and marked and arranged. Everything labelled and in its place and if you moved anything out of its place the fragile, crystalline lattice-work of his personality would shatter under the stress, spraying a wide area with a million shards of razor glass.

The first warning sign came with the newspapers. This guy had them delivered in the morning. Celine was up before him so she'd collect them to read over breakfast. After a fortnight he presented her with a bill for half the newspapers. Said she'd been reading them, she'd be paying for them. Now Celine didn't care whether they had papers or not. They were there and he wasn't reading them so she had. It degenerated to the point where he'd set his alarm five minutes before hers, run down, grab the newspapers and run back up into his room with them. When he'd finished he'd tie them up in bags and put them in the garbage.

Madness. When she'd invite people over he'd get her out of the room and ask, 'Who are these people in my house? Why are they sitting on my lounge? Why are they watching my television?' He'd go ballistic if she had people over for dinner and he wasn't notified well before. He liked a good five weeks notice. In the depths of winter she'd turn the heater on. He'd turn it off. She'd leave a light on in the hallway. He'd turn it off. These things would eat away at him. The relationship deteriorated. She started leaving on the lights, moving things around, inviting people over. On purpose. Finally, she realised she was becoming as mad as him and she moved out.

There are common elements to share housing everywhere. Like the shopping basket overburdened by detergent, rice and pasta. But the detergent never gets used. And the rice and pasta never get eaten because nobody remembers to get anything to go with them and if you do buy some good food for a dinner party and you turn your back on it for five minutes it will disappear and you will serve up the only stuff left, the rotting week-old salad refuse at the bottom of the fridge.

I have trawled through three states and a swarm of human strangeness and I have to say, I've seen some weird things: flatmates who like to put trips in your beer; flatmates who only ever eat expired stocks of packet pasta; flatmates who like to hide in the bathroom and watch you take a piss. Actually one guy did all of these things. Kelvin. Liked to lie in the bath in the dark late at night. I'm in there one night, tackle out, taking care of business when I look to my left and seize up in horror because Kelvin is lying in the bath with a big lurid grin on his dial. Been in there for ages. Lets out this really sick giggle. I had to piss outside after that.

This is the sort of thing I think of when I think of Brisbane. Not sunshine, or the beach, or a beer off the wood at the Breakfast Creek. Nuh.

I think of a place where anything can happen, or nothing. Disintegration, entropy, the long mid-afternoon of wanton unemployment. Wallowing in cider and children's television. I think of coming home to find some anorexic Goth woman sitting in the bathroom with her wrists open to the world explaining that she wasn't serious. 'I just wanted to see what it would be like.' Or the house which broke up over the issue of who owned the plastic dinosaurs. I lived with these two intense young girls. Painfully thin, pallid, humourless, small-breasted Smiths fans, they were. But mad house-nazis. We had a kitty for buying muesli and tea bags which the girls enforced with fists of iron. The trouble started when one of them discovered that if you saved up seven box labels and sent them to Uncle Toby, he would send you a plastic dinosaur egg in the mail, which you could pop open and transform into a baby dinosaur. The house broke up because Maud the blond Goth saw Danielle the black-haired Goth walking around with this egg dinosaur going, 'It's mine, all mine', and Maud exploded because the box tops were purchased with the kitty money. The dinosaur, she said, belonged to the house. But Danielle insisted that it was she who had saved up the box tops, and she who had filled out the coupon, and she who had posted the whole lot off to Uncle Toby, who owned the dinosaur. The dinosaur was hers. It got really ugly. There was a lot of slamming doors, a lot of note-writing, a lot of sulking, and the whole place just went down like a huge ship, bow up, slowly disappearing into the arctic sea.

When I think of Brisbane I see a lot of these wasted spider people dressed in black. It was like the lost Valley of the Goths. Still is. These people don't seem to realise that when Robert Smith minces about in his black clothes, he's performing on stage, under a lighting set-up that's much more amenable to the streamlined form than some blocky boy in the hot sun of a Brisbane afternoon, wearing black stretch Lee jeans with that slight shininess around the arse and that creasing of the crotch which comes from a lot of wear without a wash. These guys, they're strictly public service nowadays – Social Security, Veterans Affairs, Valuer General, that sort of thing. But their lifestyle hasn't changed. Smoke before work. Beers at lunch. Buckets after dinner.

We all smoked way too much. If you took all the shit we smoked in just one year and rolled it into one big joint, it would be so much bigger than the biggest joint you have ever seen that you would need to smoke two really big joints just to deal with the concept of its incredible bigness.

Marijuana culture is developing regional styles. Elements of the culture, the language, the implements and the product itself, are readily transferable. You can get good and bad smoke everywhere (except for Melbourne where you only get the bad stuff). The poorest smoke will encourage you to watch daytime TV and wish that your flatmate would walk to the corner shop for another packet of Tim Tams. The best smoke will peel your head like a fat Bondi orange, pour rainbows through your eyes, punch out the seven veils of consciousness separating this world from the next, and make you wish your flatmate would walk to the corner shop for another packet of Tim Tams. Joints, cones and bucket bongs are found in all cities. But at the level of attitude and rituals, cultural differences are manifesting themselves as different signature themes in the cities of Australia. Consider the bucket bong. It's very popular in Queensland, much less so south of the Tweed. Every house I've lived in and visited in Brisbane had a bucket bong stowed away beside the brown couch or sitting in the laundry out the back.

The thing is, the bucket bong is a complicated arrangement, not lending itself to quiet reflective smoking, and not easily dismantled in times of crisis (*Open up Birmingham. We have a warrant.*) Worse still, it's not very dignified. You sit in a circle on the floor taking turns at plunging your head into a bucket of water while sucking on a very large plastic bottle. After my first encounter with the bucket, where I had eight cones by mistake, I fell into a plastic wading pool and remained there until late in the evening.

Perth and Brisbane have taken to the bucket bong as though the desire for it had lain within them like a disease. Sydney and Melbourne have not. The tyranny of distance can't explain this failure, because its popularity has leapt directly across the continent and into the lounge rooms of the West Coast. Why would such a difficult technology, one not at all amenable to subterfuge and the fast getaway, find ready acceptance in the repressive environment of Queensland but not with our bohemian cousins down south? I think this is style fascism again. The important thing in Sydney and Melbourne is not to be seen to be stoned. It robs you of your cred, and cred is the only thing people understand in these two cities. This would explain why my attempts to introduce Sydney to the bucket have been greeted with polite bemusement, and why nitrous oxide is the accessory of choice for the serious young dope smoker in Brisbane. Nitrous is a really short, really intense high, a little bit like amyl nitrate which has the potential to kill off millions of your brain cells in a big hurry. When you consume a bulb of nitrous, your head buzzes and the ceiling breaks up into a mosaic of coloured squares and triangles of light. It wears off quickly, however, usually after about 30 seconds. But if you pull a cone beforehand, the high lasts about three times longer and is a bit more intense. A man in the grip of a nitrous binge is an ugly sight – a vision of helplessness, laughing hysterically at nothing, slobbering and thrashing around on the floor. But nobody cares about your cred in Brisbane, because nobody has any of their own. It's just that big extended family thing where everyone knows everybody else's secrets.

It took me two or three months on the Sydney share house circuit before I realised the drug of choice in this town was heroin. Everybody had smack in their past. It wasn't cool to be shooting the stuff up at the moment, but a long ride on the Horse was an absolute must for the fully rounded hipster's CV. People just couldn't tear their eyes away from the fabulous anti-glamour veneer of it, even in the Cross and Darlinghurst where you could see the real smack fiends – the drop-lidded, floppy-jointed, spastic horror street junkies with their pinned eyes and terrible skin

– junkies who imbued blasting up with all the fashionable cachet of eating a cold, half chewed Big Mac from an unguarded industrial bin. Madness disguised as style fascism. A big worry.

While Melissa was living at Kippax Street, I came home a couple of times to find these smack fiends draped around the living room, whacked off their nuts. Came home and discovered a couple of them in there by themselves once, with Melissa nowhere to be found. It felt good toeing them in the ribs and telling them to get the fuck out of my house, knowing they were incapable of dealing with the world outside. They left uncomplaining, shuffling out the front door in slow motion, squinting up at the fierce December sun.

There was something in it though, the addiction to anti-glamour. As much as they inspired contempt, the junkies weren't all that far removed from me. When Jeffrey went belly-up in front of the television, I'd been living in share houses for ten years. I'd been ripped off, done wrong, burned out and scammed in every one of those years. I'd lived in one or two nice places, but mostly they were pokey, airless flats or houses on the verge of some major structural failure. My beds were foam slabs on the floor, my cupboards stacks of stolen milk crates. Even when I began to write for glossy, well-paying porno mags and the average balance on my keycard crawled into three figures, I needed that continual injection of bizarre and unexpected strangeness you can only get by living with a random series of complete strangers. Tent-dwelling bank clerks, albino moontanners, nitrous suckers, decoys, wonderbabes, gay blades, vampires, mental cases, acid eaters, mushroom farmers, brothel crawlers, fridge pissers and obscurely tiger-suited Japanese girls. I had become the chaos around me – I'd wake up sometimes, stumble into the bathroom and just stare at the palid, hairy, red-eyed horror looking back at me in the mirror. I realised that I too was a rider on the endless highway ribboning through the madness of it all.

The cops did a quick search of Jeffrey's room while the ambulance guys tagged and bagged his sorry carcass downstairs. They found some old fits and foils and left it at that. Told us to stay out of the place until they sent a science guy around to do the job properly, but I pulled his room apart when they left, and as I explained, struck gold the third place I looked, the battery compartment of his ghetto blaster. Found the money. Close to a grand. He was a dealer, then. Probably would have worked out of home. No great loss.

But as I stood there in the living room, Jeffrey's money in my hand, staring at the green bean bag and the yellow police tape on the floor, I felt my own mortality for the first time. I looked at the crumpled bank notes and thought if ever there was a moment to get out, to dive head-first through the window of opportunity, this was it. I made a promise to myself to do something. Anything. To seize the day and get a life.

But in the end I bought the house beers and pizza and that weekend we had a fantastic party. Hired a band and everything.

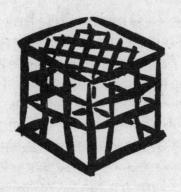

ACKNOWLEDGMENTS

First off, I have to thank all of my friends and former flatmates who spilled their guts. Jim Anderson (Seen the milk, Jim?), Luke Berry (You sure about this job?), Launz Birch (It's easy Launz. All you need is a word processor and $5000), Samantha Boucher (Who loved you babe?), Brett Cheney (Splitter!), Granger Cooley (Gentleman farmer), Toby Creswell (Don't come any closer Geoffrey), Amanda Curties (You picked it up?!!!?), Anna Deykin and Anna's cool flatmate Margi (It'll be fine. She's between boyfriends), Jon Dwyer (See you in alt.sex.badger), Helen Field (I'm telling you, it's all true), Robbie Grehan (Hey there! Beautiful day), Bob Heather (Is she little, Bob?), James Hine (Did I listen? You'll never know), Shelly Horton (The Romans had the right idea. Throw 'em to the lions), Brett Kunkel (Has anyone seen Kunkel or Birmingham. Anyone? You Evans? Or Moriarty?), Brett's mate Robin (Hey, there's a girl called Jenny looking for you), Chris Linton (Come on. Who was it?), Jillian Lye (Did you just hear something?), Jane Lye (I'll chase away the burglars for you anytime), Peter McAllister (Gonna eat those veggies Pete?), Rudolph Hess McAllister (He vass never in der Ukraine), Des McCawley (It made sense. Honestly), Corina Mackay (If she calls the lawyers, let me know), Jed McNamara (You done much defamation law, Jed?), John Manion (You gotta lock 'em in the first few nights), Susan Mansfield (What is that smell?), Adrian Matthews (I never thought of doing that with a scooter), Sarah Mulveney (The rich are soooo much weirder), Andrew O'Dempsey (It took me two bottles to finish this), Scotty O'Keefe (Send in the Decoy), Craig Roach (I'll bet you're still eating that shit), Peter Rohen (Then, fuck me dead, he showed us his arse!), Howard Stringer (Actual teeth marks?), Perri Timmins (Actually, I sprayed some on them on purpose), Heather Vaile (Who's my special girl?), Clinton Walker (I ever tell you how I crashed Mason Stewart's computers?) and Danielle Wilde (Allo Allo). ¶ *From the final frontier;* Tom Milledge, Wayne Sowry and Dave Kinsella-Holmes. ¶ *For that crucial last minute technical assistance;* Zoe Chan and Paul Fraser. ¶ *For all the whiskey and money;* Michael Duffy. ¶ *And for devotion to the cause above and beyond the call of duty;* The angry, Macintosh-punching Peter Rohen, the relentless, red pen-wielding Howard Stringer and the poor old long suffering Heather Vaile.

THE TASMANIAN BABES FIASCO

John Birmingham

Sequel to *He Died with a Felafel in his Hand*, this
novel is the story of seven days in a shared household.
When JB and his flatmates take in the new guy they have
their doubts. The Celine Dion albums, the hordes of fluffy
stuffed animals and the plastic-covered floral-pattern
love seat should set their threat detectors singing.
But nobody is paying attention.

Within days their house has become a swirling
maelstrom of death metal junkies and Drug War narcs,
stolen goods and hired goons, Tasmanian Babes, karate
dykes, evil Yuppies, dopey Greens, and the Sandmen
of the Terror Data.

Now the flatmates have one week to sober up,
find two thousand dollars and catch the runaway new
guy before Pauline Hanson, the federal government, cops,
crims, their landlord and some very angry lesbians tear
their house down and stomp them to jelly.
Can a bunch of hapless losers hope to defeat such an
unholy alliance?

ISBN 187589 188
Duffy & Snellgrove